Homesteading on the Knife River Prairies

by Pauline Neher Diede

Pauline N. Diede

edited by
Elizabeth Hampsten

with an introduction by
William C. Sherman

and drawings by
Stella Fritzell.

Published under the auspices of
Germans from Russian Heritage Society
1008 East Central, Bismarck, North Dakota 58502.

To:

My children and grandchildren, that they will remember the merits of pioneer America, and to my father and mother, my uncle and aunt who lived it, to my sisters and brother, my cousins and all Knife River area homesteaders, I dedicate this book.

IN AMERIKA DURCH GOTTES GNADE
In America through God's Grace.

Copyright © 1983 by Pauline Neher Diede. Second printing, 1984. Third printing, 1989. Fourth printing, 1992.
Printed in the United States. All rights reserved. Except for brief quotations in critical articles and reviews, no part of this book may be reproduced in any form or by any means, electronic or mechanical, including photocopying or recording, or by any information storage or retrieval system, movie, dramatic, television, motion or talking picture purposes without authorization from the holder of these rights without permission in writing from Pauline Neher Diede, Box 108, Hebron, North Dakota 58638.

Nor can anyone sell my books without paying royalty to the holder of this book.

Published in the United States under the auspices of the Germans from Russia Heritage Society, 1008 East Central, Bismarck, ND 58502.

Book and cover design: Kim Yeager.
Photos in the possession of Pauline Neher Diede.

Acknowledgements: Some of the material in this book has appeared in a rather different form in columns by Pauline Neher Diede called "The Prairie Echoes," published in the Hebron (ND) Herald, Jane Brandt, owner and publisher. Support for the preparation of this volume has come from the University of North Dakota English Department, Journalism Department, College of Arts and Sciences, and funding for photocopying from the Faculty Research Committee. Publication arrangements are made with the assistance of Karen Retzlaff and Dr. Armand Bauer (Chair) of the Publications Committee of the Germans from Russia Heritage Society. Printing by Kathy and Rodney Grantham, East Grand Forks, Minnesota; production by Plainswoman, Inc., Box 8027, Grand Forks, ND 58202.

Text set in ten-and-a-half point News; titles in Artcraft.

ISBN 0-685

On the cover: The children of Uncle Fred and Aunt Sophie Martin, about 1915: George, Fred, Emelia, Lena holding Albert, John, Martha, and Henry. Martha and Albert were born in North Dakota, the rest in South Russia.

An Introduction
Time is Running Out

Germans from Russia are a quiet people. Although more than a century has passed since their coming to the United States and Canada, and although their descendants now number over a million, until recently few Americans had heard of Germans from Russia, perhaps because they chose to settle the Great Plains' most rural regions. Or perhaps their obscurity is due to their being hard workers who dwelt without fanfare in small towns and simple farms. For a long time no aspect of their life attracted the attention of scholars or of the wider American public.

Only in the last decade have English language publications begun to outline their special past: Joseph Height's two volumes, **Paradise on the Steppe**, and **Homesteaders on the Steppe** (both published in Bismarck by the North Dakota Germans from Russia Heritage Society, 1972 and 1975); Adam Giesinger's book **From Catherine to Khrushchev** (Battleford, Saskatchewan: Marian Press 1974); and two journals, **The Heritage Review**, a quarterly of the Germans from Russia Heritage Society, and the **Journal of the American Historical Society of Germans from Russia**.

Thanks to such works, it is possible now to understand the significance of Catherine the Great's manifesto of 1763 which turned the eyes of thousands of German citizens eastward in hopes of acquiring free land. The manifesto set forth conditions by which German farmers and craftsmen might acquire free land along the Volga River and later in the Black Sea region. We can trace the migrations of numerous caravans to Russia in subsequent years. One can appreciate something of the hardships of German families as they fashioned new villages from a raw frontier. Their emerging prosperity and subsequent discouragement are reflected in the way Russian authorities alternately aided and suppressed the activities of these colonists. Today we also can feel something of both the excitement and the perils of that later movement that began as a trickle and became a flood—the surge of Germans seeking land, freedom and opportunity on a new frontier in North America.

However, so far the German side of the story has been better told than the North American, for the primary sources of German-Russian information are the Landsmannschaft der Deutschen aus Russland archives in Stuttgart, where scholars have focussed on the group's experiences both in their German homeland and in the Russian villages. Comparable gathering of materials about their lives on this side of the Atlantic is just beginning, although the shortage of published American records is understandable. Germans came from Russia to this continent with meager resources, and without wealth or an educated professional class. More importantly, the first years of prairie life were busy times; survival came first and left little opportunity for the luxury of writing or publishing.

The one expression of German-Russian culture that did record life in a personal way has been story telling, and it is from this tradition that Pauline Diede draws the life of her father and mother, uncle and aunt as precious memories of the past, the heartaches, hardships, and first successes of a German-Russian family seeking to establish a new life in one of the most difficult parts of America, the prairies of western North Dakota. Pauline Diede fills an historical void. Seldom has anyone detailed so well the confusion in some German immigrants' minds as newcomers confronted an Anglo-Saxon world. And seldom if ever has this early struggle for survival been described by a woman. Pauline Diede's narrative is exceptional in revealing more about the details of women's lives than do most public accounts. Here we see what many have suspected, that the wife and mother was forced to pay a harsher price for the decision to relocate in the New World than did any other family member.

The story of the two families Pauline Diede describes is both typical and unusual. The Nehers, her father's forbears, were part of a minority group, Separatists, actually Chiliasts. (Pauline Diede calls them Baptists, but that name comes a generation later.) They went initially from Germany not to Bessarabia in the Ukraine as did many other Germans, but to a more remote region, the Tiflis area of the Caucasus, and they came to America by way of Montreal instead of through American seaports as most Germans did. The Neher and Martin families then settled in Mercer County late, a full twenty years after the influx of the first German land seekers; by that time the best land had been taken and only poorer acreages were left. Also unlike other German-Russians, the Martin and Neher families located in what we would call a mixed ethnic neighborhood and were thus deprived of the mutual support of friends and relatives, a support that carried other families through the difficult initial years. Also contrary to the practice of most other immigrants, the two families arrived not in the spring but in autumn. Winter was to punish them for such recklessness.

Pauline Diede bases her description of events in Russia on bits and pieces of family lore filtered through generations of Russian and American living. Fragmented and possibly distorted by family perspectives, these nevertheless represent the shape and sounds of the past of a particular family. But her story is more than personal. Passed on in such an oral fashion, it embodies something of the culture and ideals of many, perhaps most German families of similar Russian background. Old-timers will recognize the sadness and tears of departures, the harsh moments of the first plunge into the new prairie world, the yearning for the security of Old World village life, the kindness of neighbors, the hopeful spring planting and alternating success and failure of harvest. Small items have an authentic ring: the "Knife River Irish," "brauchens," children working for sometimes harsh neighbors, digging a well, bake ovens and root cellars, camomile tea and pumpkin turnovers, and the long wagon journeys to market.

An interesting question remains. Was the demeaning position of women portrayed by Pauline Diede typical of German-Russian families? Some observers say not. But here again the scarcity of historical information limits our insight. An understanding of the role of women in frontier America, whatever the ethnic tradition, is still largely a matter of conjecture. (How many people realize, for instance, that one-sixth of the Nehers' neighbors who filed homestead claims were women, and that proportion was not unusual in western North Dakota?) Pauline Diede at least introduces the subject of women's position in German-Russian settlement culture.

Somewhere in old trunks and back closets exist other accounts of German homestead life awaiting publication. Surely the memories of old-timers in prairie towns and retirement homes contain the raw materials for family memoirs. Besides giving us an historical document, Pauline Diede's work ought to provoke other similar endeavors. Time is running out and we need them badly.

— William C. Sherman

Foreword
Eavesdropping Behind the Door

I see my father, Ludwig Neher II, pacing back anf forth from one corner of the kitchen to the other, telling stories about life in Russia. He loved to talk about his ancestors and why they left Germany to migrate to Russia. Often he would stop walking and gaze at the ceiling, his eyes half closed, thinking about the past, homesick especially for his mother. Growing up, I listened carefully to those stories. When a letter arrived from a relative in Russia, Aunt Sophie Martin would read it, and often when I huddled down on the floor by the parlor door, I would be sent away, for it was not nice to be that curious. But five or six decades later, I am glad I was, so that now I can write the story of my immigrant parents.

This story is based on the experiences of homesteading both the Russian steppe and the American prairies, and while it concentrates mainly on two German-from-Russia families—those of Fred and Sophie Martin, and Ludwig and Christina Neher—it also touches on the story of all Russian-Germans, "Russland-Deutschen," who settled in South Russia in the late eighteenth century and then emigrated to America beginning in the 1880s. Sophie and Christina were sisters; Christina was my mother. Together their two families totalled 12 people, a smaller group than usually emigrated together.

Listening to my father's stories at parlor gatherings, I learned of the frightening experiences of his father and Grandfather in Russia and of their 2,000 mile trip from Germany to Russia. I learned of their lives peacemeal, and eventually had several lengthy discussions with my father about the Neher forbears, his own growing up, and the first years of homesteading in America. I took notes, and told my father that one day I wanted to write this story, at which he appeared pleased. Three months later he died. In my sorrow I dreamed of him incessantly and determined to write out his story.

Time, I realized, was vital. I visited also my Uncle Fred Martin who with his wife Sophie had made the trip to America with my father and mother, and lived also in Hebron in those years. I found Uncle Fred very preoccupied caring for Sophie, then an invalid suffering from a crippling stroke. Those were sad times. After Aunt Sophie died, Uncle Fred was more ready to engage in interviews. I can hear him say, "Du, Poulie, hascht so-aa arge interazant in unz Roosa-Deitsche. Warum?" (You, Pauline, have such a keen interest in Russo-Germans. Why?) He chuckled through tears but was glad and cooperated well, the more so as he always had thought that Russo-Germans were not valued enough.

One of Uncle Fred's sons said to me, "I never realized my father had so much story in him; he never talked about old times to us." I explained to George that I had kept after his father for answers, that I was after a continuous story of his life, and was surprised by what a clear memory he had. Only when I asked Uncle Fred about his marriage with Aunt Sophie would he not open up, but he spoke readily about his orphan life in Russia. He had been driven out of his father's home by his stepmother at a very young age and forced to hire out to work to survive. After he reached a marriageable age, he told me, he worked at the George Steinert farm in Groszliebental and there married Sophie Steinert. He was reluctant to talk about that, and I later discovered that their marriage, like my parents', had been an arranged affair.

I had many visits with dear Uncle Fred before he died. They were good interviews and I took many notes. He spoke mainly of the journey to America, their first winter in Ashley, North Dakota, and the beginnings of homesteading in south Mercer County near the bend of the Knife River in what was called Elm Creek. He went into great detail, explaining every activity of a project. He told me the story of Tillie's birth, how both families suffered through the first several years, the problem of getting sod houses built, and the difficulties of getting enough water, fuel, food, and clothing.

My mother also spoke to me, but briefly, of these experiences. Another source of information before my birth was Pauline Jaeger Birkmaier, who gave me detailed pictures of those times of poverty. She said to me, "Your poor parents had two babies and a third one coming that was premature (that was myself). I had to help out as a hired girl with no pay. I couldn't exist under those conditions for too long, If my mother had not helped out in many ways, it could have been tragic."

Additional information came from two neighbor ranchers, the brothers Matt and Jack Crowley. They had given up ranching and were retired when I visited with them about their early lives. Jack's answers to my questions were short and abrupt. He told me my mother baked the best everlasting-yeast bread in the whole state of North Dakota, but on the whole, Jack had not been fond of his Germans-from-Russia neighbors. Matt recalled more sympathetically my parents' years of poverty: "I loved those little girls when I entered that sod-hole home, and I pitied them. It nearly broke my heart to see such dire needs, and that is why I supplied your parents with their first horse and cow, and moved my horse plow over to your homestead and broke up their first field. That is why I ventured over there with my mower to cut feed, even though I had many responsibilities right at hand here on the ranch." Matt was a wise and compassionate man. Jack had a sterner temperament and had been rather oblivious to the needs of Russo-German immigrants, yet during the course of our interviews he mellowed and realized that my people had had much harder times getting started than had the Crowley family. Jack had been a true frontiersman, knowing well how to manage to survive.

I hope that all these sources will make the reality of these lives as clear to others as they were to me listening to stories from the earliest days I can remember.

I The Neher Family in Russia

My family was part of the restless and dissatisfied peasantry that lived in the area of Germany named Swabia. European peasant history is the history of people of low social rankings, the mass of the population, those who turned the soil, strewed grain by hand, gathered it and stepped out the grain from sheaves. They were the grassland people who took seriously the parables of the Bible. They were German colonists who settled on the great and vast steppe of Russia's new soil. They were hard working people, my people, the Germans from Russia, who cultivated not only Russia's steppe but also America's vast prairie land.

By 1818 Germans in the Odessa Valley had made a good start at building villages and breaking the steppe for plowing, thanks to government allotments to buy such essentials as oxen and a hand-sharpened plow-share attached to a rude frame. But times were hard. There never was enough fuel, no such thing as coal, and not enough trees for wood. Had these Germans known about the lack of fuel as well as about other hardships, they would not have come. But once there, they did not have the strength or the means to turn back, and had to survive the best they could, and they did, half-starved and weather-beaten. Babies were born into cold and hunger and many died.

Immigrant life in the Odessa valley was particularly hard on women. They suffered not only the usual deprivations of cold and hunger, but in addition were subjected to the violence of cold, hungry, and desperate men. Many a pathetic story has been told of a woman hitched to a rough wagon filled with clothing and food, with a wailing child on top of the load, and a four- or five-year-old running along beside, the mother pregnant as well. Miscarriages were common, and women bled with nothing to wipe themselves. They resorted to bunched dry grass or shaggy leaves. Women ran to hide in shame and often found no hiding place, subjected as well to the ridicule of men.

By the time my great-grandfather Jacob Neher arrived in the Groszliebental area of the Odessa valley (fifteen years after the first settlers), conditions had improved somewhat, for the

Russian government was providing more help in response to the many deaths among previous colonists. But Jacob Neher like others found the available land to be of poor quality, yielding meager crops. In addition, the family was repeatedly struck with deaths of children, as one after another was buried in a hole and covered with clay, the little graves filled with clods ("bola") as was the German custom, and wild flowers or sweet smelling herbs planted at the graves. Crosses were made of tree limbs or woven reeds, and the corpses wrapped in coarsely woven reed pads. This latest grief made Jacob Neher all the more determined to leave South Russia, and his family joined others in a move 800 miles further east, crossing the Caucasus mountains. Jacob was a strong Baptist and became a leader of that caravan. After a long and treacherous journey, during which they lived mostly on rabbits and wild berries, they eventually settled in Katharinental, a largely Catholic village.

Here, about 1826, Turkish and Kurdish horsemen descended upon the colony of Katharinental and murdered local villagers as well as Baptist colonists. According to a missionary's report and word from a few who escaped, houses and fields of grain were burned and gardens destroyed, young women and wives were sexually attacked, and some were torn away from children and husbands and forced into slavery. The marauders tied screaming children together and threw them over wild horses. They tied old men to the tails of wild horses, and tied other adults, mostly women, to the trunk of a tree and burned or killed them on the spot. The name of the village of Katharinental became known for this terrible massacre.

A few of the young men escaped to the next village, including one or two Nehers among whom may have been Jacob Neher's eldest son, also named Jacob. What the orphan Jacob's life was like after that is not known, except that he settled in Govillags near Tiflis. One of his sons, William Neher, was conscripted into the Russian army during the Crimean War in 1853. He was killed, leaving a family. He had a son named Ludwig, who, when he heard of his father's death, decided to return to the place of his forbears across the Caucasus mountains, back to the Odessa colonies. This Ludwig was single when he joined a small group of Baptist families who eventually reached and settled in the Groszliebental area, by then one of the more prosperous and fertile regions of South Russia, where the Russian government had helped to develop farms and stone quarries. By the mid 1800s

Groszliebental had become the largest and most prosperous of the Odessa colonies, and it was from here that many colonists who later went to the Dakotas originated, Sophie Martin and Christina Neher among them.

Thus, in the 1870s Ludwig Neher and his Baptist wayfarers settled in the colony called Freudental, where the land was of better quality than the hard gumbo that Jacob Neher had originally been allotted. But Ludwig I still was not happy; he was restless because Catholics and Baptists argued so much about scripture and ritual. One day he entered the home of a Baptist minister and found a family desperate for food and clothing. Typical of pastors' families, they nearly starved for doing as the Good Book said about taking in wayfarers and giving them bread, even if their children were left with practically nothing to eat. Here Ludwig met the minister's daughter, Julianna Zimmer, who was anxious to get away from the destitute conditions of her family. She married Ludwig in the hope of a better future, having had her eye on the more established colonists who had more to eat and were better dressed than any pastor's children. She felt that Ludwig came from what she called "families of the earth breakers." To be sure, turning over sod and planting seed so far had been Ludwig's lot, but he was never satisfied with staying long in one spot, and was always looking for a better place to make a living and a better religious atmosphere with other Baptists. Not surprisingly, the Nehers remained poor, and Julianna after marriage found herself not much better off than she had been in the home where she was raised.

My Father's Boyhood

Once married, Ludwig Neher I and Julianna (my grandparents) settled in a minor "dorf" (colony) called Sofiental in Bessarabia. As the colony was in its early stages of development, Ludwig obtained work at meager wages constructing winter huts. This was not what Julianna had wished for. She wanted to settle in one of the more developed colonies where she might become a land-owner's wife, helping to plow the grassland, strew seed, and reap harvests so that her family might have ample food, clothes and a warm house. But she never realized her heart's desire, for Ludwig found no higher position than building houses of clay, including one for themselves, for which Julianna was thankful.

Their first son, my father, was born there in Sofiental on October 14, 1882. Soon after his birth, the family moved to Karlstal, a resort closer to Odessa, a beautiful place sheltered from Russia's raw winters, where the soil was unusually fertile and gardens and grape arbors flourished. Wealthy Russian noblemen used Karlstal as a retreat, building elaborate houses of quarried stones. German colonists lived on the outskirts of these estates, producing grain, hogs, and dairy cattle for the wealthy families. Ludwig Neher I was hired as caretaker for the gardens, and this is where my father spent his boyhood. It was a picturesque place he remembered. Grape vines hung over whitewashed houses. There were apple trees, a scarce fruit in those days, which my father craved. The family lived in a two-room clay-wicker house on the outskirts of Karlstal, close to the street. More babies were born to the Nehers and several died of plague, but as each was born following a death, that child was named for the one who had died. The surviving children were Ludwig II (my father), Jacob III, Wilhelmina, William II, Anna, and Daniel.

Ludwig's job in Karlstal as a boy was feeding hogs and watching over the hog pen. In the fall, the Neher family was given one large hog for butchering (if they needed more meat, they had to buy another hog). What Ludwig remembered most about those "hog days" was the stench. The hogs were fed over-ripe grapes, fallen half-rotted apples, cabbage leaves and soft onions, so no wonder they smelled. Ludwig gathered the nobleman's house garbage for the hogs and there got his lunch from pretty good apples that would have been thrown away, and in that manner satisfied his hunger.

It rained a good deal in Karlstal, making the hog pen a place for hogs to burrow in mud. When the wind was from the right direction, the air, one's clothes, everything smelled. Ludwig remembered his mother suffering from these offensive odors. Ludwig often was scolded and flogged by the hog overseer. One day he ventured to ride a boar, who darted right through the wooden fence, followed by all the other hogs, all running through the streets and rubbing off their grime on white-washed houses and ruining garden patches and orchard treelings. That day Ludwig got a flogging and his mother cried for him. It was also the day he learned the art of white-washing houses, part of his punishment. In later years, Pa's hog stories brought out his sense of humor, although he wondered also whether his mother then did not wish herself back in a poor minister's household.

Ludwig described his growing up as being among hot-tempered "smart-heads" and "fat-bodied fuedal superiors," and always felt he had been under the influence of harsh scoldings and frequent beatings, and a rule that swallowed up his sense of personal identity. Ludwig retained most of his life the habit of indulging in emotional outbursts of temper toward neighbors and family members, whom he was apt to treat severely. However, at times the influence of his mother's tenderness would show through and his high, order-pitched voice would come down, and he would talk in a milder way with an infrequent word of praise.

A woman in those days had few rights and kept her needs to herself, often in desperation crying out her troubles only to another woman, though cautiously so, that she not be discovered in her laments. Ludwig spoke often of his mother with tears in his eyes, overcome by emotion and homesickness so that his statements were short as he let out a sob. What he remembered most about his mother was seeing her on her knees praying, her hands outstretched to the Heavens where God was. Julianna Zimmer had a hard lot, as did most women in those days. But somehow she gathered the grace of endurance and patience and taught her family to follow her "Heiland" (Lord). She gave her children something else as well, good minds and an incentive to learn. Even though her children were denied school, Julianna taught them scripture and how to read and write German.

Ludwig remembered his mother hardly having an idle moment, always working with food, weaving, mending, knitting, gathering and shelling grain, and doing all the jobs women were expected to do. When Julianna had a bit of time, she would teach her children scripture and German. She brought up six living children: Ludwig II (my father), Jacob III, Wilhelmina, William II, Anna, and Daniel, several other children having died.

Ludwig seldom spoke about his father, the gardener, although he gave the impression he thought him a determined and courageous man, and boasted often of the leadership qualities in the Neher line. In Karlstal his father was under the rigid discipline of military guards whom he was obliged to obey in spite of their cruel ways. Even so, colonists in Karlstal, as in Groszliebental, Johanestal and Freudental, prospered well. The colonists' hard work, thrift and creativity brought prosperity to New Russia. Throughout the 1880s and 1890s schools, churches, and craft businesses thrived, and families dressed and ate better than ever before.

In the summer of 1903 Ludwig was impressed into the army to fight in the Russo-Japanese War. Cossacks had been riding through village streets picking up young men without serving them notice. Mothers cried and screamed at them. Ludwig hardly had time to say good-bye to his mother and gather up a few belongings. His mother shoved into his bundle the warmest pair of underwear, and Ludwig often said later that if it had not been for those underwear, he would have frozen to death. Military training was not very rigorous. Ludwig remembered doing things as clumsily as he could, purposely bungling everything. He was assigned to the kitchens, and found that cattle in feedlots were treated better than soldiers. One day his job was to get the sauerkraut out of the barrel. It was a hot summer and worms were crawling through the kraut, but when he described the mess to the cook, he got a blow on the head and orders to cook the worms with the kraut. For the rest of his life my father hated even the smell of sauerkraut.

He served about a year, through a record cold winter and an especially sweltering summer. He saw two of his buddies killed, and another severely wounded, whom he carried to a pond. Here he washed his friend's wounds and fetched him drinking water in his cupped hands. Ludwig often spoke of that man's miraculous recovery, for after two days and nights in their hideout, a peasant woman appeared, as out of thin air, dressed in rags, bringing a kettle of cooked grain and a spoon. She came from a village nearby, and must have heard their moans. Adam Wolf, a Catholic, was the soldier's name, and he and Ludwig kept up their friendship after the war and emigrated at the same time.

When Ludwig returned to Karlstal, he found his father too ill to continue working in the Count's courtyard, and the family moved to Freudental. His mother Julianna had aged much, and the second oldest brother, Jacob III, and the youngest boy Daniel were readying themselves to migrate back to the Neher homeland in Germany. This was all very hard on Mother Julianna, although she was a woman of foresight and knew the future in Russia was bleak for her children. She did not want them to suffer as she had and so did not discourage them from plans to immigrate elsewhere. Political disturbances became more numerous as colonists' villages and families were divided in their opinions about revolutionary measures. More and more German natives sold their belongings and headed for America.

Ludwig was now of marriageable age, and approached the village marriage broker whose business it was to keep track of suitable young women. When a girl's breasts developed and she had become well trained in indoor and outdoor labor, she was ready to be married. It was thought a disgrace for a younger sister to be married before an older one, so some marriages were apt to be hurried. Ludwig's marriage broker took him on a rough wagon ride from Freudental to Groszliebental to call on the George Steinerts. There Christina was home, busy shoving bread out of the clay wall oven. The bread was light and smelled good; Ludwig ate some and liked what he saw of Christina. A week later the two were married and settled with Ludwig's parents in an already overcrowded household, but Julianna was good to the bride.

These were my parents, Ludwig II and Christina Steinert Neher. My oldest sister Matilda was delivered by Grandmother Julianna and consequently received a bit of cuddling from both grandparents, although the last love embrace came all to soon, for Ludwig, Christina and baby joined Christina's sister Sophie and her husband Fred Martin and their seven children on an immigration trip to North America.

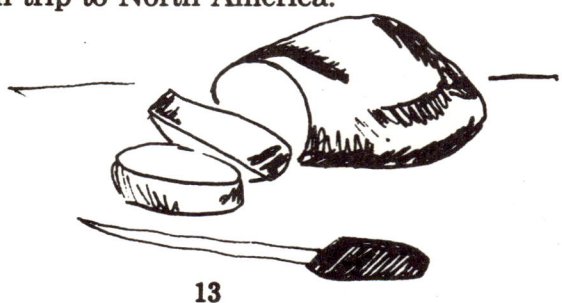

II Uncle Fred Martin's Story
Summer: Russia to Canada by Sea

Uncle Fred Martin told me the story of the immigrating experience of the two families. The Martin family consisted of Uncle Fred, Aunt Sophie, and seven children: Magdalena (Lena), almost a teen-ager; John; Fred; George; Henry; Mathilda, two years old and sickly; and Emelia, a baby of a few months. Children often were named for older family members, resulting in two Mathildas in the Martin and Neher families. In the late summer of 1909, both families sold all their property except for a meager supply of clothing, bedding, kitchen utensils, and food. Uncle Fred's family had a fair supply of money to start with, but Ludwig Neher, partly because of the interruptions in his life caused by his stint in the army, was poorer. What follows is my uncle's account of the two families' migration.

We tied our essentials up in bundles or stuffed them into sacks and loaded everything onto wagons along with the eight children and four adults. Everyone knew that good-byes to relatives and neighbors were final farewells. Tears, hugs, kisses. The village minister read the Word of God and prayers were in screams: "Gott sei mit Euch" (God be with you). The Steinert family was very much opposed to having Sophie and Christina and all their grandchildren taken so far away. The Steinert family lived in the most prosperous of the German colonies, Groszliebental, and were considered well to do, even able to afford servants during the busy seasons. Their church was the pride of South Russia and their children had had the advantage of a schoolmaster. Sophie thus was reluctant to give up these advantages. I, on the other hand, had been an orphan and very poor, and Sophie felt that I was beneath her. She had married me unwillingly, and unwillingly was obliged to obey and follow where I might go. I knew that although emigrating meant going into the unknown, it also would mean greater security for my boys and a way of avoiding their conscription into the Russian army, reason enough to take the venture even against my wife's opposition.

It was easier for Ludwig to decide to go. He could see that his family had suffered enough from wars and he had not yet established deep family roots. His mother was broad-minded and wanted her war-weary son to settle in America. In fact, she wanted to join him there, but her ailing husband stopped that idea. Julianna knew how poor her son was and that she could not help him much. Christina received her dowry in material essentials, and the family was off, knowing they would not see each other again. The well-trained team of horses obeyed the crack of the whip. There was a last look, the waving and sounds of "At-ye, Gott sei mit Euch" (Goodby, God be with you), the last look at Russia's steppe as the wagons rumbled toward Odessa.

At the Odessa train station everything was unloaded. There other emigrant families were waiting for the train; a good many of the onlookers were looking for a way to steal something to eat. Such a picture of destitution. We German emigrants looked on them as outlaws, lazy Russians, gypsies, and we took care to safeguard our belongings. The train was crowded, as bad as a stock car of hogs. Children were perched atop sacks and bundles so closely they hardly had elbowroom, and they set up a howl. The palms of their hands were saucers into which was thrown a piece of bread and "schpeck," or salt-brined pork. No washing allowed, for water was not to be wasted. No toilet facilities except on the premises of a train station. Children rebelled and cried and were shoved, shouted at and slapped, even more by train conductors than by parents. I even felt like slapping my wife because she constantly scolded me for choosing this ordeal for the family.

After ten days of the crowded, noisy, and filthy train, we arrived in Hamburg, Germany, where we were driven into a steam filled room. According to rules, we were stripped of our clothes and washed down with disinfectant to kill lice and any sickness we Russo-Germans might have brought with us. Clothes were thrown into a large boiler and two women with massive wooden sticks punched the clothes up and down. The boys bawled for their clothes. We pushed them under a large canvas cover and told them to stay there. Just outside of the fumigating room were wire clotheslines for clothes and bedding. We hoped for sunny drying weather; if it rained, it would have been too bad. You stayed and suffered with only a blanket, and I didn't know what we would have done with the naked boys if it had rained. Two kindly German women gave the older boys and Magdalena a gown with snap fasteners. Lena was embarrassed and ashamed and cried a lot.

In Hamburg, Martins and Nehers boarded the ship. I do not remember the name of the ship. I was too concerned with immediate worries and hoped for a healthier situation on the ship than what we had had on the train. Our two families were allotted three third-class rooms on the bottom deck. Martin children were given the larger room. They slept on the floor on a sawdust mattress. Immigrant families were crowded everywhere, along with boxes and barrels of supplies. Everything smelled badly. Everywhere you turned, you bumped into someone or fell over a bundle. It was pure havoc. One or another of the boys was bawling most of the time, especially George. It took a lot of impatience for me to hit a child, but one night I had had it. In anger I got up, struck a match and lit the kerosene lamp on the wall. My eyes focussed on the ceiling quite accidentally and I saw a mass of crawlers squirming and creeping into crevices. I examined George's body and found bedbugs crawling about, his body covered with red blotches, and then I knew why he was crying. We were not able to get another room, for there was none to be had. We left the kerosene lamp burning all night, considered an extravagance in those days, but it kept the bedbugs away.

Conditions in the lower deck were terrible, not only for the Martins and Nehers and their children, but for all other emigrant families. The stench of urine and vomit, slimy overcooked food, and crawling bedbug and cockroach infestations all were getting too much. Sophie had stopped scolding; she had no more energy, for our two littlest ones wore her to a frazzle.

One day a storm hit the ship. For the boys, it was exciting, and before I realized it, they were on the top deck pushing each other into the massive waves that splashed onto the deck. I caught one of them just in time before he was washed into the sea. I was at one of my weakest points on the entire journey. I shivered from fright. I stood on deck with my hands and arms outstretched shouting "Gott, bring' uns doch zum land" (God, bring us yet to land). I didn't know where to go, for I was terribly seasick. So were many others. Children were screaming and vomiting. When the storm ended, instead of us all being thankful that we were alive, we were humped over in despair. This was the time I wished we could have turned back. I felt guilty that I had brought my family into such an ordeal. My spirit was at its lowest ebb.

To add to our hardships, we had a sick child. Our two-year-old Mathilda taxed everyone's energies, especially those of our teenage daughter Lena. The child's cries turned to wails and we knew she was losing strength. I asked God that if our child was to die, He should preserve her life at least until we could bury her in the earth, for all deaths that occurred aboard ship resulted in sea burial.

As the storm subsided, one little boy on the edge of the deck went into convulsions and died. Little Andrew was forceably taken from his screaming mother and his body put into a gunny sack. To console them, one man showed the bereaved parents a **handful of dirt which would be sprinkled into the sack on little** Andrew as the captain uttered the consoling words, "Earth to earth, dust to dust." Yes, there was more dirt in the box, and I wondered whose body would be sprinkled next. I thought of our little girl. Your Pa read scripture to console the mourning frightened parents of little Andrew. He was good at that. He was always thankful his mother Julianna Neher had taught him to read the Bible.

After the storm and sea burial of little Andrew, I could not have been in lower spirits. I was not only irritable but frightened, and so were all the rest in that jammed hole of the ship. What difference did it make that God had taken little Andrew from all this suffering? But I did not want any of my children buried for a whale's meal.

During the sea voyage we had more than ordinary wind. I hardly think we had one calm day and I didn't have an hour's good sleep the entire time on the ship. Such a jamming of people and cargo in the lower compartments and what foul air there was. Sickness broke out. A few children got the measles. Lena was expected to keep the boys in line. She discovered some of the boys had lice in their hair. No wonder they cried most of the day and night: bedbugs, no room to romp, not enough clothing, and lice on their heads. I had had a rough growing up. My mother died when I was very young and my stepmother was mean to me. I begged often for a piece of bread from our dorf meighbors. But as I watched what my boys were going through, right then I felt they had it even worse. At least when I cried, I could run and run with footing on land. Even spending time at the back yard pig pen in Russia was better than this. The pigs didn't seem to mind if I grabbed an apple that wasn't quite rotted. People can be more cruel to children than to animals. They called it discipline. I too got hard with my children at times, but then I remembered my hard lot as I grew up and decided my children needed better treatment. Then I would cry and become tender, wipe dry my eyes and hope again that in a few days we would step onto American soil, but we didn't know what the unknown land had in store for us.

Most immigrants on the lower deck were farmers from Russia. Two Hungarian families on the other end broke out with measles. Emotion ran high. Even if we differed in religious faiths, we had one thing in common—hope for a better land for our children and ourselves. I heard lots of scripture that related to the promises of God and loud prayers all through the day. Your Pa was a great one for that. Sometimes I envied him because I couldn't read as he did. However, I had more money in my flat leather pouch than he had in his. I had it tied around my belly, under my underwear. Every move I made I felt it, and to me that money was security.

I have to mention one other act common around the congested ship, and that was the habit of spitting. Every male adult did it except Ludwig and me. Children had constantly running noses. These things turned my stomach almost more than anything. The days of sea life spelled devastation, both to my spirits and to my physical well being. Our Mathilda was fading in health. I could see that. My wife was worn out and distraught. Oh yes, it had been my idea to drag my family of seven children away from pretty comfortable conditions in our Groszliebental home to an unknown America. Ordinarily a ship crossed the Atlantic in nine or ten days, but this took well over two weeks. The steady wind hampered the ship's speed and pushed it off course. Even the ship's crew scoffed and became belligerent. It seemed immigrants from Russia were treated worse than other Europeans. We were the down-trodden, and felt it.

Autumn: Montreal to Ashley by Land.

The ship arrived at Montreal, Canada, during the night, and we had to gather our possessions, bundles and sacks, and try to keep the family together when time came to debark. I did not feel excitement but anguish. The children looked pale and wandered about in a straggly manner. Two of them were running a fever and we knew families had to go through inspection. If any family member was afflicted with disease, you were sent back. A woman at the other end of the ship had lost her mind, and I knew the family had no chance of getting through. I looked at that man's cross, and considered mine light. Both our families passed inspection, and no one took notice of Henry's flushed face. He was breaking out with measles. Your father wrapped him up in a blanket and carried him to the port's camp, where we were stalled for a number of days. A U.S. inspector discovered our trouble and said, "For measles you would not be sent back to Europe. Keep your family here. Do not take them on the train in this condition." We were delayed for over a week and were lodging in a ship's tent from which we could see the Atlantic Ocean to the east, but I kept my eyes focussed to the west, where land was. One of the first blessings was milk for the children, and another was their being able to run free. What a relief, yet what an uncertainty!

After the excitement of loading all their possessions, the Martin and Neher families settled in a west bound train. What a luxury this train was, even if it was packed with immigrant families. It was much more comfortable and much cleaner than the one we rattled on from Russia to Germany, and the autumn scenery was spectacular. The vast land gave us revived hope for better things. I felt both hopeful and deeply concerned. Things were getting harder for Sophie. Our little girl was not getting any better. I sensed her days were numbered, yet I was thankful we did not have to bury her at sea.

The next lay-over was Chicago. The wait was not that long, but with a sick child, time seemed endless. A good elderly immigrating mother who wore Russian clothes came to our assistance; at least we thought she could help. She gave our little Mathilda a good smear with homemade ointment that she had brought from Russia, and she uttered a meditation and exercised the child's opposing legs and arms together, releasing bodily tensions. Then she wound a wide cloth around her abdomen, admonishing us to cover her well for a sweat. It did Mathilda some good, as well as the rest of us, for she fell asleep and slept and slept. At times I felt our little one would be better off to sleep into eternity. First I had prayed that God would spare us a sea burial; now I prayed that God not let our child die along the road, and surprisingly the Good God answered my prayer.

Another train took us westward, through Minnesota into North Dakota. I had never imagined the United States was such a massive country. The train sped on and on, and the scenery changed. I was in a sort of trance, frightened of the unknown. One of our greatest hardships was not speaking English, and most conductors and depot agents were of Scandinavian background and could not speak our language. We could not speak high German, which was more commonly understood. As soon as we opened our mouths, we gave ourselves away, we were "Rooshens." The one consolation was that there were quite a few of us Germans-from-Russia immigrants, and that gave us a feeling of company, although we felt inferior.

Ludwig showed the conductor an envelope with an address in Eureka, South Dakota, where we wanted to go. Your Pa knew a few English words, so I left him to handle arrangements for our destination. But when the train stopped in Medina, North Dakota, the conductor forced our families off the train. There we were, with everything we owned on the platform of that prairie town station. Those were frightful moments for us. I realized our families depended on Ludwig and me to take us someplace where we could sleep and eat. We were told to find a livery man who would haul us by horse-drawn wagon to our destination, Eureka, South Dakota. The boys started to run about as though they felt the open spirit of the prairie town. We felt the usual commotion of uncertainty. What next? Where were we going? I walked toward the depot and as I leaned against the corner of the railroad station I cried to God to help us. Little did I realize that the Provider in Heaven already was at work.

Your Pa had met with another German-speaking man, who out of curiosity had been watching the action on the depot platform. He spoke a similar low German brogue, and I assumed he was Catholic. He directed us to the town livery stable. The livery man made a living by hauling immigrant families to their destinations with horse-drawn wagons, and he divided us up and found invitations for us in several homes overnight. They were Catholic people, but the women made no fuss, for they were all religious people. Their homes seemed to us fit for a king's family. Pictures of Holy Mary and Jesus hanging on the cross adorned the parlors of these homes and I wondered whether that was something we could look forward to. Must we be Catholics to become so prosperous? We had not had such good tasting and satisfying food since we left Russia. The children got fresh cow's milk. Is that what **America promises us? Oh, thanks to God. We** Protestants were brought up to keep our distance from Catholics, but I tell you, we were pretty glad these Catholic families took us in that day. I felt the love of God in them.

The next day we packed our possessions and children into the livery man's wagons and hitched his well-fed horses and started south. This was the first time I was relaxed enough to focus on the prairie land. It was rolling plains country with homesteads perched about, showing patches of turned-over prairie soil, indicating that the land was being farmed. We **traveled as far as Ashley, North Dakota, where the livery man** decided that was as far as he planned to go. We found ourselves moved into a train boxcar. Again, kindness was shown to us in our hour of need. Immigrant people were all around us, and God, how we thank them.

Winter: In a Boxcar

It was fall in 1909 and we realized we had better stay put. We were told winters could be pretty rough. Luckily we found a flat-iron cooking and baking stove. We soon realized that on the treeless prairie land there was no fuel to feed that stove for the winter. We sent the boys out to gather "mischt," dried cow manure, but it was scarce because everybody was gathering it. Your Pa managed to beg a load of fresh manure from a farmer. We handled it as we had in Russia, working in weeds, twigs and pieces of wood to make dried fuel cakes that we stacked close to the door of the boxcar so as to keep watch on it. We also were introduced to some new fuel possibilities, dried corn cobs, that we had not had in Russia. Your Pa had a way of making himself acquainted, whereas I felt inferior because words did not come to me as easily as to Ludwig, for which I envied him. One day Ludwig disappeared for hours and turned up with a box full of crude grayish black pieces of something I had never seen before. It turned out to be substance from a top layer of coal. Despite the heavy smoke we realized that that was what we needed for the coming unknown winter. Somehow your Pa saw to it that we had coal piled on the other side of our boxcar home.

The next necessity was food. With twelve of us, we needed a good supply of everything. We sorely needed help, and if it hadn't been for those loaves of bread that good people gave us, things would have gotten unbearable. Our boys had a way of running about and showing their hunger. Some of the more established immigrant families realized our dilemma. One day our oldest son, John, brought me a large hunk of fresh bread soaked in chokecherry syrup, and it was good. The next day a good woman brought us a big kettle of borscht the way we made it in Russia. It was not long before we had several German-from-Russia friends. Even if they were still poor, we felt a longing to be in such a settled position. We thought that if America gave us what they had, we would be thankful and satisfied.

We were two families crowded into a rectangular boxcar for our first winter in America; we were jammed into every inch of space. The bedding we had lugged with us had to be burned because of bedbugs. People rescued us with a gift of fresh corn husks and straw for filling large sacks to serve as mattresses that we placed in one corner where the two sets of parents and three little ones slept. We managed to make a hide-a-way nook with gunny sack cloth around it. In it stood a five-gallon empty grease can which an Ashley farmer had given us as a night toilet, and near it a box of corn husks for toilet paper. We thought that a luxury. Corn and a certain wide-leaved sudan grass were new crops that fascinated me. We had none in Russia. Only better established farmers dared raise corn and sudan grass. What a challenge.

Your Pa was a fast pacer and one day walked out to a prosperous farmer who had brought us a load of corn husks and sudan grasses, and to his surprise, found the farmer to be a hog raiser. Ludwig bought a huge fat hog and a beef and fortunately the farmer allowed us to butcher, make sausage, and place the pork in brine all at his place. He even allowed us to smoke the **sausages, some pork, and hams in his smoke house. What good** people they were. So many people helped out. Certainly God provided and answered our cries, for we needed so many essentials. We hardly knew what need to handle next, for our little girl was getting weaker. One grandmother and midwife supplied herb treatments and gave the child the sign of the Holy Cross, a healing belief in the Catholic faith. We Protestants used the method we called "brauching." In those days when our little one was waning in strength, I realized that the Catholic people showed a concern that made their religion seem good and right, even though our religion had said they were wrong. God had a reason for bringing us together for closer understanding of each other's religions.

Our oldest daughter, Magdalena, then a teenager, had played the role of an adult since she was a child, for we placed weighty responsibilities on her. In those days, it was customary to expect the impossible, especially from a girl. Lena had to watch the younger ones, often acting severely. So many of us crowded into so small a space caused friction. One evening Lena was lifting her very sick little sister from one arm to the other when the child's body went limp, the ebb of life gone out. Little Mathilda had died in Lena's arms. "Yetz hasht Du das kind erloest, O Gott" (Now you have rescued our child, Oh God). It was a hard night, especially for Lena. Much as Sophie and I did not want to part with our little one, we had expected her death. Your Pa wrapped the corpse and took it some place; where, I did not ask. I later found out she had been placed in a back yard fodder nook that contained husked corn and ground oats and was next to a pen with a grunting hog in it. The same good Catholic family that had invited us over for paprikash and fresh bread now helped us get the coffin made. The good man gathered wood from someplace and before long nailed together a box big enough to lay the child in; his good wife made a cushion for her to lie on—acts of sensitive generosity.

There was an American school in Ashley. We saw how lively the children in the school yard appeared, and we thought we had better get some of our middle boys started. Fred, our third child, would be the one to start, for we needed Lena and John to help gather manure fuel and dig coal for the oncoming winter. Lena placed a hunk of bread and an apple in a syrup can for Fred's lunch. He was told not to eat the apple before noon, the one incentive to get him going. But Fred barely reached the school ground when some older boys piled on him and called him a "Rooshen." Fred knew not a word of English and had no way of defending himself, and so arrived at his boxcar home beaten and bawling, less from bruises than from having his apple taken away. Both the apples and a few syrup pails had been given to us by our generous American Catholic friends. Poverty and the lack of variety of food kept growing children always hungry and quarrelsome. The biggest squabbles among boys were over stealing each other's apples. They were plain starving for lack of nutriment.

Boxcar life could get fairly hysterical, worse than a coyote hole. Your mother was pregnant and threw up a lot, and the little food to spare for us adults was not enough for our wellbeing. We lived on fat meat, bread, and strudel with hardly any vegetables except for the crock of sauerkraut that the Catholic family had given us. Your mother could not tolerate fatty foods nor the sauerkraut. I often wondered that the baby she carried lived through it. It must have been the grits she ate before going to sleep that kept the baby alive. Our boys knew the town from one end to the other and had a way of getting a stick of peppermint candy, an apple, or a piece of kuchen. John was good at that. Once in a while he would beg for a whole kuchen which he sometimes shared. In those days we slapped the children a lot, when really those poor children were not mean but half-starving. Lena grieved much for her little sister. We had to get rough with her and force her to go to school. Your Pa and I clashed a lot. He had that Russian military aggressiveness that got to me, but yet I was glad he went ahead with so many of his ventures.

I think the journey to America and that first winter in Ashley were the hardest times of my life. I got into the habit of crying much of the time. Sometimes I was glad it was your father who disciplined the boys, for it relieved me, but his military Russian ways affected all of us. Your mother was especially frightened of him. Ours were the kind of arranged marriages that were proper in those days. Many couples hardly knew each other. Your mother and father were an example, for neither knew more about the other than first impressions.

The winter passed slowly. December was rough, and so was January. If only we could get out of that hole. The children had running noses all the time and at Christmas we all had a fever. An Ashley midwife treated us with teas and garlic plasters, and what an odor that made in the boxcar. When I took ashes from the stove I often laid some hot ashes onto a shovel and sprinkled sugar on it, causing a blue-red flame and a swirl of white lime smoke that was supposed to be a disinfectant. That helped a bit.

A Trip to the Bismarck Land Office

In February 1910 we experienced a chinook. We were ordered to get going for Bismarck—Ludwig and I, that is. We were to contact the land office to obtain land to homestead. Most of the land close to towns was already taken up, meaning we had to move farther west than we had hoped. Not knowing how radically the weather could change in North Dakota, Ludwig and I were dressed comfortably for a hike. We set out for Bismarck, knowing that we would have to walk most of the way. Our aim was to get as far north as the railroad, then catch a freight car the rest of the way to Bismarck. With our bread and sausage we were ready and were warned to take along a heavy coat, what they called sheepskin coats. I had bought one, but your father couldn't afford to. Ludwig went about ranting in his high voice for someone in Ashley to lend him a coat. The livery man found an extra sheepskin hanging under a harness in the livery stable. We were amazed that anyone could be so rich as to own an extra coat. Only in America.

It was time to leave. Sophie and Christina were to take responsibility for the boxcar. Our hike northward was pleasantly interrupted by an occasional wagon ride for a mile or two. How I wished we were as settled and well along as the many homesteaders along the way. I prayed a lot. I wanted God to hear me. The chinook weather held up for several days. At Medina we caught a freight train, joining other bums. Two things I remember about that freighter. We saw ferocious sun-dogs. Secondly, the wind had gotten suddenly cold, and as your Pa dozed off to sleep, a bum stole his bread bundle that one of the women had packed for each of us. The bum devoured it so fast that Ludwig could get none of it back. We were mighty cold when we reached Bismarck and hurried to the depot where a potbelly stove was throwing off ample heat, so much so that it glowed red. This was a sign for a change in the weather.

Your Pa complained loudly. He was cold and hungry. I couldn't share much of my bread for I too was hungry. I couldn't help it if he let the bum eat his bread. Suddenly Ludwig left the depot and disappeared. I knew if anyone could find food, he would. He found a store with a kerosene light flickering at the back, so he pounded on the door. The storekeeper answered impatiently but opened the door anyway. Well, Ludwig got fed and brought back something to make a drink, Ovaltine, a powder that was to be mixed with water. None of us had ever tasted anything like it. The storekeeper told Ludwig it was a drink for pregnant women, but we drank it, pregnant or not. The next morning, after sleeping on the depot floor, we saw another new thing, snow. The depot man told us that he knew the storm was coming.

The storm raged for nearly a week. I had never, in all my days in Russia, seen anything like it. It was a good thing the railroad company had stored plenty of coal chunks to keep that potbelly stove going. Your Pa and I slept on the floor, close to the stove. Our caps were pillows until Ludwig managed to get a few gunny sacks from the storekeeper. We used everything to make the floor less hard and drafty. Even the depot man stayed put to watch the premises. A number of freight-train bums joined us, which aggravated your Pa, who had not forgotten what one bum did to him.

As for food during this blinding snowstorm, we almost starved. I think it was the livery man who managed to bring a kettle of cooked grits, and we took turns eating with the few spoons he also furnished. We were like hungry pigs around a trough. Snow was melted on the stove for drinking water. Once the storm let up, Ludwig disappeared again, and I knew either he'd get lost or he would appear with something to eat. He had courage. This time he made his way over to the grain mill and elevator. Sure enough, the miller supplied him with an ample amount of grits along with a couple of cans of sardines. Nowhere in Russia was food preserved in a can; this was new to us. The depot man opened the sardine cans with a sharp knife and poured the contents into a dish. All this went on in the freight room, out of sight of the bums. Of course, grits were beginning to steam on the potbelly stove top, and all of us, including the bums, got all the grits we could eat, but we did not share the sardines. That was something Ludwig and I had never tasted before, and it did our stomachs much good. We even saved the can. I knocked the sharp edges smooth with a stone and we had the little container for all kinds of uses.

The snowstorm days dragged on. Fortunately we had been alerted to take along our sheepskins or we would have frozen without them. As the storm gradually receded, your Pa took to his feet and knocked at doors of Bismarck homes, bringing many a loaf of bread back to the depot. So then we had bread. We managed to get to the land office to find that the only available lands for homesteading were at quite a distance to the northeast from Richardton, close to the Knife River. Most of the land close to towns already had been homesteaded. We were too late for the best choices, for large numbers of European immigrants had already settled before 1910.

The only family I had known anything about were the Walths, near Richardton, so I bummed a ride on a freight train to Richardton. It was terribly cold; I wrapped one gunny sack around my head and another around my feet. Ludwig made his way back to Ashley, also part way by freight train as far as Steele. From there he walked, making his needs known at every homestead farm. Of the two of us, I knew he was better at finding food and short sleigh rides. Someone had to look after the train car families: "Ach liever Gott, erbarm dich doch ee-ver unsere not" (O Dear God, have pity and know our needs).

"Unser Herr Gott hat mich khoert" (Our God did hear our pleas). The Richardton depot man saw to it that I got to the Walths, people whom Sophie had known something about, and I was taken in with open arms. O, that good soup that soothed my hunger. The Walths also were Germans from Russia and had immigrated some years earlier. Seeing their plentiful food, clothing, and comfortable home, considering the times, my whole being surged with new hope. The two-room sod house was firmly built; the larger room even wallpapered. On the wall hung a calendar with almanac showing signs of the phases of the moon and other figures I could not understand. There was a picture for every month and a number for every day. I almost fell over when I was told they got this calendar from the drugstore, free. Was this what America had to offer?

There were three beds in the Walth's rectangular sod room, and in the fourth corner a potbelly stove. I slept in one bed with two children on a straw-stuffed mattress that rustled. But the pillow under my head was soft. I had never before slept in such luxury. During the day the beds were made up and covered with patchwork quilts, and on the parents' bed was a bedspread with a nubbly design and fringes, deep tan, a bed cover I thought fit for a king. What elegance. I began to hope that life in America would also favor us in such a manner, but for now I wished only for a roof over my children's heads. I did a lot of praying, and crying.

The next day, Mr. Walth hitched two horses to a sled. Under our feet he placed two stones wrapped in grain sacks that Mrs.

Walth had heated. She also put a loaf of bread and some cooked side pork into a round can. The day was clear and cold. I depended on Walth's judgment. All I knew was we were sledding over rough country. You could see settlements here and there with smoke coming out of stone chimneys. We even spotted some one-room lumber shacks. We made it to the Jaegers and unhitched the horses. Brother Walth put horse blankets on the two greys and led them to feed. I was baffled by uncertainty about everything and wished the aggressive Ludwig were there to push decisions.

The Jaegers spoke High German, having come directly to America from Germany. I felt inferior, for their talk showed they had had more schooling than I. They had class, and I began to understand how many people had come from other European countries besides Germans from Russia. Frau Jaeger reheated some "schpaetzla" soup, and how it warmed my whole being. I had with me a hand-drawn map of what prairie land was still available for homesteading. Mr. Jaeger knew a lot about the layout of the land, but I could not understand him. We both spoke German, but our dialects were different. Just the same, I gathered that he did not want me to squat on land adjoining his homestead, even though there was some available that looked good, in my judgment. He took us on a sled ride further north into rather hilly country and decided for me where I should begin taking up a homestead. I insisted that we select a place to put a sod house or dugout for our families. I was at a loss. I knew a decision had to be made, and so we posted the spot we felt suitable for a dwelling. We were satisfied that there was plenty of land to the north and northeast for the expansion I knew we needed.

Things began to fall into place. Brother Walth encouraged us to put up a shack instead of a sod house, for if I wanted to buy land and homestead further on, I could move the shack. I was fortunate to have Russian rubles to change to U.S. greenbacks with which to purchase necessities. Most Germans-from-Russia immigrants were not that self-sufficient in money. That is, my family and I had lived through pretty good times in Groszliebental. When we sold our belongings the dorfs were prosperous. But your father and mother had hardly anything. I wondered how they would make it. On top of everything, your parents were expecting their second child within a few months. I did not allow myself to worry about how things would turn out.

The days following that severe blizzard of February 10, 1910, were very cold. In spite of all, I accomplished much, especially planning, but if I had not had help from the Walths, we would have had to stay in Ashley to find work or other aid. Helping out was a must in those days. People understood that if a wayfarer asked for bread and a place to lay his head, it was a holy obligation. Anyone who did not respond to the needs of others was judged harshly in strong language and fitting verses from the Bible. There was a closeness among Germans from Russia homesteaders. They took it as their mission to share bread with the hungry even though they had little for themselves. They thought themselves inferior to other settlers, and they stuck together.

During an early spring chinook, I got myself back to Ashley. "Ach liever Gott, wenn ich dra denk" (O God, when I think back). Ludwig bought a 350-400 pound hog. For the second time we butchered, made sausage, and rendered lard in that farmer's kitchen. Side pork and hams were placed in barrels filled with brine. These good people, also Germans from Russia, furnished us with the necessities of life.

March: Moving to the Homestead

The winter of 1909-1910 passed and March arrived. We had a lot of sickness in that boxcar, not just one at a time, but several of us at once—a dozen small and large people packed into that rectangular train car. Again I must say thanks to the good people who gave us herbs, teas, goose lard and liniments to smear the sicknesses away. We adults broke out with boils, especially around our necks, and did not have enough cloths to tie around our necks. Ludwig asked the druggist for something to heal boils, and brought home a can of carbolicsalve. What a smell! But it did the trick at least for a while. Today a dietitian would tell us we were not eating right, which was true. In addition to sickness, we had to battle another plague, familiar on the ship, bedbugs from a second-hand bed we had bought in Ashley. We had to burn the mattress as well as several straw mattresses. Your mother was highly disturbed. She could not tolerate anything crawling. What a turmoil.

By spring it was time to move our two families and few belongings to Richardton, where the Walths were expecting us, and for the trip I had bought a team of draft horses, harness, and wagon. We knew it would be a slow trip of many days. We did not figure the trip in miles, for we crossed country wherever we were told of a shortcut. The more established homesteaders were our greatest blessing. During a general spring rain of several days, we found refuge near Elgin in the granary of a family named Roth. They gave us all the milk we could drink, for they were milking by hand a cowshed full of cows that had freshened. On the other side of the barn was an enclosed place where Herr Roth had the calves binned. At the Roth homestead I had my first experience in America of sticking two fingers into a calf's mouth to help it suck up milk. I remember how I longed for my family to be so fortunate as to have milk and daily bread and such housing as the Roth family had. They too were our kind of people, Gemans from Russia, and naturally helped out where they could. The day we moved the loaded wagon out of the sod barn, we arranged children and wives atop the wagon. Mrs. Roth fed us a last meal of dumplings and potato soup, and gave us fried pork and a half dozen loaves of bread to take along. We started with a wagon load of supplies and human beings, wheels sinking into the saturated prairie road. We took turns tramping alongside the wagon to lighten the load for the horses.

We headed northwestward cross-country, with directions for crossing the Heart River. Homestead farmers helped out along the slow moving and treacherous way. The little children cried. It helped that the bigger boys could romp along and throw an occasional dirt clump at the horses to get them prancing faster. The oldsters were cranky, to put it mildly. What a trip. We were eternally thankful to the Walth family, who had been my wife's friends in Groszliebental and had immigrated some years earlier. The way they had prospered gave me hope, but how I longed to be settled with my restless children and discontented wife. "Wir waren, ach, so ungeduldig. O Gott, vergev uns doch" (We were so impatient, O God, forgive us).

There was a spring thaw, and predictions of another snowstorm made me fearful, for I did not want to experience again what I had been through in Bismarck. It turned out we got a heavy snowfall, which everyone said was a good thing. A couple of families helped us out by taking the boys and feeding them. Your Pa made himself acquainted with a Catholic family and moved in. Your Pa liked to argue religion, and I wondered how they got along. But we felt unsettled in Richardton, like parasites, eating, as we were, at others' tables. I say it was the providing God that inspired families to help out, or we would have starved. A kettle of "paprikash" soup was a favorite Catholic dish. We were introduced to all kinds of new things in America, including foods, all made from scratch, of garden produce. Every family had a large garden or two of turned-over prairie soil fertilized with manure. One was a "bashtaan," or row garden, of potatoes, watermelons and pumpkins. The good supply of stored vegetables in root cellars in the Richardton area made me hope I could provide as well for my family.

April and May: First Home, First Birth

One-room wooden shacks scattered on the prairie were signs of their owners' prosperity and were put to a variety of uses: a cowboy's refuge; a camping place for farmers during seeding and grain storage in harvest; school room and place for Sunday worship. Our family managed to acquire something that was a little more than a shack, an abandoned house, and we moved in for a while. It was April and time for spring seeding, so the first and most important thing to do was to break up some prairie for planting grain. I don't know what we would have done without the help of the Jaegers and the Maerschbeckers. I felt always that "Herr" (honorable) Jaeger was a master, and I followed his every admonition, and he seemed to want to be treated that way. Certainly I felt inferior, more so than did your father, who had a way of hollering back. With Ludwig, silence was not golden, and he gave the true Germans to understand that we had just as much right to homestead here as they did. However, we could see that the better land was going to the "true" Germans and that we were the "unwanted" and subject to their mercy. Even if the Jaegers pushed us farther into the northern hilly and stony country, I realized we had better succumb, for we needed all neighbors regardless of class or nationality. In addition, Frau Jaeger happened to be the midwife for the area, and Ludwig would need her to deliver their second child. I told him more than once to hold his mouth, we needed the Jaegers.

Sure enough, on May 6, your mother began to have labor pains, a sign that a midwife was needed. It was a beautiful day, almost like summer, but we could not enjoy the balmy weather because we had a thousand concerns. Ludwig took my team of horses and wagon to get Frau Jaeger. We were hoping the birth would take place during the day, but it didn't. The bigger children slept in the wagon. There was a thunderstorm brewing up from the northwest; we did not know yet how severe North Dakota storms could be, and not even Herr Jaeger expected the likes of a summer thunderstorm in May. We were unprepared. The older children were crowded into the wagon box at night, and I paced around outside telling the boys to go to sleep. The two littlest children were in the shack, along with Sophie, Ludwig, and Frau Jaeger. Your mother was screaming in pain, and thunder and lightning squalled with an occasional crack. We could not go into the shack, so Lena, the boys and I huddled together under the wagon and sat on a "stroh-sach' (straw-filled cloth case). Luckily we had the old horse blanket the Walths had thrown in when we left them, and now it sheltered us in that downpour. We put our heads under it, but it didn't take long before we were sitting in water. The boys bawled, and Lena was screaming in fright, she, who usually was the one to stand as a brave scold to keep the boys in shape. But not that night. This is how Ottilia (later called Tillie) was born. Your Pa always said that North Dakota's first thunder-storm brought her.

I need not describe that night. We campers were wet to our skin. We hitched horses to the wagon and drove the drenched children to the Maerschbeckers, and again our good Catholic neighbors helped out by keeping the children for a few days. I sent along some of the grits I had bought in good supply, and must admit that if it had not been for that ground grain which we could boil up in a few minutes to feed the dozen of us, we would have starved. The Maerschbeckers did what they could, and so did the Jaegers. I remember Mrs. Maerschbecker bringing over pumpkin turnovers. They had a root cellar full of garden things.

The Jaegers did an awful lot for your folks too. Frau Jaeger delivered the baby, and she did not stop there, for she realized the need all around. Mathilda was still a baby as well. The Jaegers let the Nehers move into their summer kitchen shack. It even included a stove. 1909 had been a good year for gardens, and Jaegers had a root cellar full of potatoes, pumpkins, beets, carrots and what-have-you. I felt a tinge of envy that your father had fallen into that kind of luck. I am only human. Yet all in all, it was the dear God that did not forsake him, for Ludwig had so little money, and there was nothing for it but people had to help him out, your parents had so little to start on. Not only did we have no help from the government, but we knew nothing about the rigors of North Dakota weather. We had already discovered that nature could have cruel surprises, like the soaking night of May 6. We hardly had enough clothes for a change and no place to dry them, no wash lines. Ludwig came up with a technique used in the Russo-Japanese war, spreading garments over coulee bushes or large stones. They absorbed the sun's warmth and their outer roughness did for clothes pins. What with daytime sun and breeze, clothes dried in short order.

The Beginning of a Farm

The spring of 1910 was our most difficult time as pioneers on the prairie. I hardly slept. My temper was short, for I realized my family's survival depended on what we could grow on the land. Sod had to be torn up and over-turned and grain gotten into the soil if we were to have bread. At every turn there was a need. I cannot describe our dilemma. I had bought a plow in Richardton but lacked horse power, since all homesteaders just then needed their horses to get in their crops. I cried to God for help. Your Pa had a way of getting his needs known and taken care of, and he got help from Matt Crowley. Mr. Crowley broke up quite a piece of prairie where Ludwig could take some of the sod and build a sod house, and the rest of the better land he could strew grain on.

And yes, God answered my cry too. I was fooling around with the two oxen that Jaegers had sold me, when suddenly over the hill came Matt Crowley with a good breaking plow and three draft horses hitched to it, and in no time broke up a good patch of prairie land. Sometimes I felt like wringing Ludwig's neck, but that day I almost kissed him. He knew a few words of English and somehow made himself understood to the Irish-English Crowleys. And on the way back to Crowley's ranch, Ludwig even **managed to get Matt to break up another patch of his 'hohe'** (high land). So he was ahead of me again. It seemed to me his poverty repeatedly worked in his behalf, but I was eternally thankful anyway that Ludwig saw to it to have some of my homestead prairie land broken up.

Most of the grain seeding we did by hand that first year. But by late May both your Pa and I got some oats and a little barley seeded with Maerschbecker's drill, and again I must utter a thank-you to our good Catholic friends. Both the Martin and Neher families managed to get out a "Garta-Bashtaan" (yard and outer yard). Established homesteaders shared garden seeds and some of their spare potatoes, pumpkins and other vegetables that they had in abundance in root cellars. We buried potato peelings and some pumpkin seeds in the last furrow of the field that Crowley broke up for us. The overturned sod should have been disked, but we did not have such equipment. Mr. Walth had given me a sharp spade and shown me how to get the boys to use it as a cutting tool on the massive sods. Each boy had to take his turn at chopping and leveling the virgin soil, thus making a better cover for grain and garden seeds.

Even though Ludwig and I had had to settle for stony prairie land, each of us was fortunate also to have a piece of high ground. Often among the stony hills, you would find an occasional level valley, good for planting a grain field. Then at the foot of the hill, homesteaders put their home. Why had we settled those prairie hills? We were often asked. We did so because we were latecomers and had to take what was left, nor did we have time or easy transportation to look around. Others who had first tried settling among these hills soon left to find employment in the brick yard in Hebron. Chiefly Germans from Russia, they lived in the northeastern part of town, the rest of Hebron being inhabited by true Germans, a few Scandinavians, Hungarians, and others. Not surprisingly, northeastern Hebron soon was called Moscow.

For us as a family 1909 and 1910 were very hard years, although it was a good spring and summer in 1910. But to be spending my accumulated wealth gained in the most prosperous period in Russia, with seven children and a dissatisfied wife, spelled extreme suffering for me. I admit I cried out my tensions and worked like a beaver. I often shouted to God for help: "O Gott, du muscht helfa" (O God, you must help). I built a wooden shack in the vale of the south side of our precious high ridge so that the family could be here with me rather than in an abandoned shanty a few miles south, and I thought the sooner I got them to our homestead, the better. The boys used to run across the prairie to take messages back and forth or bring me things to eat. The boys did many other things too; they were born to toil. In those days children were not accustomed to much playing. From the time they could romp, they worked.

For the time being, the most important task was to break up sod for a house. I thought of these as the "oxen days." The two draft horses could not do it all, so I let myself be talked into buying a pair of oxen. As it turned out, the boys had to do most of the pulling of both oxen and plow. Those oxen were the most stupid, uncooperative, stolid animals I had ever encountered. I tried beating sense into them, as was the custom then. Being forceful at hitting, both humans and animals, was a part of playing the role of a man. A man could release his temper as well as show his power as boss: "Du horchst, oder ich nimm dich rum" (You listen, or I'll take you for a round). I tried practicing that on my oxen, but it ended with my having to give up, and to give them up.

The one-room shanty housed my family temporarily. Most of our domestic work we did outdoors. We set a barrel at the northeast corner of the shanty to catch rain water, and the wash tub at the northwest corner. Water was most important for our survival and we were fortunate in getting successive thunder showers. I soon found my second biggest mistake (buying the oxen was the first): the shanty sat on what became a pond. My Sophie hauled me over. Deep down she loathed everything about America and never stopped thinking about the Groszliebental life. It is odd that we even slept together, but we had no other choice. Our shanty floor was one big bed at night. There was a lot of bawling at night, particularly the night we had several inches of a downpour and the floor gradually submerged in water. Everybody was up and around and in a stand-offish mood. As many as possible crowded into our bed. Some of the boys perched atop the table, cuddled into the straw mattress. I prayed it would stop raining before we went for a shanty swim: "Ach liever Herr Gott, genunk isch genunk" (O dear God, enough is enough). The next morning everything was wet, even my spirits. This was one time I considered going back to Russia, but I did not say so out loud.

Lena had banked our little old-fashioned stove with dry twists of hay, weeds, and sticks, and fortunately they were still dry. We cooked a kettle full of grits, brewed coffee with "zigory." God must have spoken to Sophie and she listened, for she had made a kettle full of borscht and had baked bread the day before the downpour. We set the borscht into the heated oven. Everything was wet and the shanty was sitting in several inches of water. I will never forget that night and the days that followed. The boys were bad enough, but Lena was the most disturbed. We were crowded together like coyotes and their young in a hole. You can imagine Lena's turmoil: she was in her adolescence, with no privacy whatever, and we did not even recognize a girl's needs. We shrugged off having any kind of conversation to explain to her the stages of human development. In those days, everything was shameful. The less said and the more children were kept in ignorance the better. Lena went through a hard time in her growing up years. All in all, we expected too much of her.

One Must Have Water

Your Pa was working on his own sod house a few miles east of us. He managed to get help from the Bittermans. Your Ma and the two little ones (Mathilda was 15 months old and Ottilia 2 months) had been living in the Jaegers' summer kitchen and missed the downpour. Ludwig had seen the thunder storm coming up from the northwest and strode over to the Bitterman place. He had a way of making himself at home wherever he laid his cap. The Bittermans also were very poor, struggling to survive in those hills, but somehow that woman placed bread and side pork into a gallon syrup pail for Ludwig and also gave him a three-gallon can of drinking water.

It was crucial to find water. Most wells were dug with pick and shovel. One of the Bitterman boys believed in the magic of a willow twig. The twig had to be held just right to respond to Nature's power, then it would move toward the earth. But you had to believe in it. I had seen it work in Russia, and we found water where it pointed.

In the wake of that storm, we not only had to move the shanty to higher ground, but also were obliged to build a dam to keep back the water between the two hills. Everybody worked like beavers. We did not even have the convenience of a stone-boat and the boys had to gather and carry stones. Fortunately I had bought a spade, shovel, and crowbar, and these tools, especially the crowbar, inched the shanty out of its stand of water. When I think of it now, I have no idea how we ever got our shanty up that hill. It took strength beyond ours.

Ludwig also was building a dam at a similar site, but he was much worse off than I, for he did not have children to help. I also had the advantage of Sophie's being here to fix meals. Even so, one item for a meal was as much as we could expect: either bread, or a kettle of borscht, but not both. The craving of little stomachs was evident. Children were denied regular meals and drinks of water, but they were expected to help with the backbreaking labor. Often nothing made sense to me, and it was a good thing that I had no time to think about it nor to listen to Sophie's reproaches. We were stuck on this prairie and had to endure it and hope it would be kind enough to produce food. We needed every stalk of grain that now was growing well after the numerous rains. There were some good consequences of those horrendous thunderstorms. They softened the soil and broke down the sod which should have been disked. We were so lacking in tools and items for changing the rugged prairies into productive farm land that when I think back to our first year on that coyote land, I can hardly keep from crying.

The gap between the north and south hills contained a nice spread of water. Sophie could now fetch water with a dipper to pour into a tub where she soaked and swished clothes. Frau Walth had given her a few pieces of homemade lye soap that helped to get out the grime. Children matched prairie wild life in how they dressed and what they ate. I remember John pulling up stalks of grain and eating the whole thing and the others following suit. He had to be stopped, for we needed to have every head of grain mature. Both adults and children craved more nutrition so badly they plucked tender grasses and chewed on them as would a cow. The boys were told not to swallow the grass, but I know they did. Their stomachs needed something, and the roughage had a laxative effect. We worried about poisonous plants, for we knew so little about prairie life and often made wrong assumptions. The boys quenched their thirst by cupping a hand and drinking water from puddles and creeks where water was filled with squirmy life, or they would simply lie flat on the ground and drink from a pool, swallowing what gave them intestinal worms. We did not have pure water and did not know enough to boil drinking water, and learned many things the hard way.

The boys ailed and lost strength, but it was not hard to guess what was wrong, as those pinworms in the intestinal tract acted up, especially at night. Mrs. Bitterman investigated. She greased her forefinger and reached into the rectum of one of the boys, grabbing hold of a nest of worms. She boiled up a bitter drink that caused vomiting, but I don't know what it was, and she advised us to go to the drugstore for worm medicine, something we had never done in Russia, where midwives took care of all ills, including worms, and it was a new idea to us to spend money, when we had so little, on medicine. The druggist was friendly, understood our German-Russian dialect, and gave us lots of good advice, admonishing us to dig a well for drinking water rather than cupping it out from the dam or creek hole, and I did not argue the point. In fact I became a regular visitor at the drugstore. The druggist made me feel better about not having had any schooling and not knowing as much as others because I was "Russian." At any rate, I had learned something Ludwig didn't know.

Yes, a well had to be dug, but where would we strike water? Bitterman was summoned to use his willow twig, and he found a location easily as some mysterious force turned the willow fork downward. If he was under some higher power, it was not the devil, that I knew, for the devil would not have wanted us to have water. I felt many times that "der deifel war lo-oz" (the devil was loose) out in those stony hills. That day I knew that God was there. We dug only 11 or 12 feet when out gushed some water. I hollered in elation, "Get the dipper and pail," and the boys scurried off. The water came fast and clear. I tasted it and drank myself full. That was one time I saw Sophie smile. It was a day I'll never forget. Of course it took some days before we had the well squared, lined with lumber and a rope and pail attached for hoisting. No wonder it was called the wishing well. The prairies could not have been developed without water. Fortunately, in every area there was someone who could water-witch; he hung around until water was found, then asked for his pay, a few pennies. Some people laugh and don't believe in water witching, but I crossed my hands over Bitterman's and experienced myself the magic pull of the willow twig, a feeling I can't describe except to say it is one of God's many blessings, a miracle of the prairies.

So went my Uncle Fred Martin's account of our family's first year.

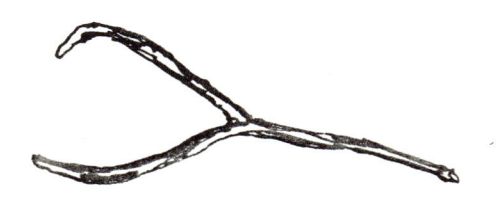

From the album

(Left) Ludwig Neher II and Adam Wolf upon their discharge from serving in the Russo-Japanese War, 1904-1905. From the Picture collection of the State Historical Society of North Dakota.
(Above) Ludwig Neher on his 64th birthday, shortly before he died.

1

2

3

) Uncle Fred Martin and Aunt Sophie. 2) Caroline Steinert, who remained in Russia; Aunt Sophie and Uncle Fred, with Magdalena. 3) The George Steinert family in Grosliebental. Front: Grandma and Grandpa Steinert; Lena Martin, John Steinert, brother of Christina. Back: Matilda Steinert, George, Fred, and Christina just before she married Ludwig Neher. 4) Elm Creek School Number 2, including 5 Neher children. 5) Knife River swim after chokecherry picking: Anne, Elsie, Ottilia, Pauline, Louise, and Clara Neher.

III. The Second Year, 1910
Help from Neighbors

1910 was a critical year for the Martin and Neher families, for they all too soon ran out of the money they brought with them. The Russian rubles Fred Martin exchanged for American money now barely took care of essentials, and at that, it was hard to reach town sites or stock markets to buy horses, a one-share plow, or a milk cow or two. And the Nehers' money pouch was nearly empty. No wonder Ludwig Neher became arrogant—he needed help and said so. He also could run faster than any other man among neighboring homesteaders, and one day, on the spur of the moment, he ran four miles to the homestead of the better established rancher Matt Crowley. Ludwig knew a few English words, and was learning more by keeping company with Matt Crowley, who caught the drift of his pleas for help with the aid of hand and arm gestures. Ludwig was an energetic talker. Crowley also knew a few low-German dialect words. He had already helped Neher plow land, and seeing him coming now, he may well have dreaded being asked for a cow and a horse. And that was what Ludwig did want, for he needed to save what little cash he had for a plow and a thousand other things.

Ever a man of mercy, Matt Crowley took Neher at his word and offered him one late-bred heifer about due to calve and a horse that could be hitched to a one-share plow. The heifer had yet to be broken for milking. The mare was with colt. I heard my father say over and over how easy Crowley was to deal with because he trusted his word, even though Crowley must have known it would be a long time before he was paid back. And still there were problems, as Crowley knew only too well, even with the aid of the new animals. For how were they to be confined without fences to keep them, or convenient water, or shelter during storms? Crowley knew too that the Nehers had very little to eat themselves and that Mrs. Neher and her children were living in the Jaegers' summer kitchen. Ludwig knew that Mrs. Jaeger would not let his family starve, but he too was hungry much of the time. His lot was even harder than Fred Martin's, for Martin had his family with him and his boys were old enough to carry sod and stones, and Sophie was able to cook kettles full of grits and dumplings to keep them going. Is it any wonder that Ludwig Neher went from one household to another in quest of a meal? Crowley noticed that he was hungry and invited him to the cowboys' bunk house for beef stew simmering on the cast-iron range.

At this time Matt Crowley was still a single man with a good start in raising horses and cattle. He had come with his parents, Jeremiah and Johanna Crowley, from Minnesota, in 1887, and he understood the harsh Dakota country. He also knew what it was to be hungry and to chew on the same buffalo grass as his pony did. "You ate when you got something," he'd say. And he knew also how much work and worry there was for Ludwig to get started. And so he let him go home with a full stomach, riding his horse and leading a prospective milk cow on a length of rope attached to a halter, and carrying a syrup-pail of well-water for good measure. The reddish-brown mare was slow-gaited, for she was heavy with colt. She was named Bay, and the cow, Bossie. Bossie was tied to the mulberry bush beside the sod house, and Bay found shelter about half a mile away in a clump of trees—elms, chokecherries, Juneberry, a gooseberry bush, and buffaloberry, with a pond of water at the foot of the hill. Neher was in high spirits that particular late spring day, and he even caught a bush rabbit for Frau Bitterman to make into a stew. He grew homesick, with tears in his eyes, remembering his mother, who would have said, "Bub, sei dankbar fur das essa" (Boy, be thankful for anything to eat).

Soon Bossie had a calf. At first she allowed herself to be milked easily. Neher sat on a stone while he milked. He felt the firm udder. Then Bossie kicked, throwing him off the stone. It took a while for the two to trust each other. After a time, Bossie made the stone her stopping place when she wanted to be milked, and Neher bragged about how clever she was, and how now he could offer extra milk to the Bittermans. He could skim the cream and make butter. Each morning he filled the syrup can Crowley had given him, had milk to drink all day, and also had enough for the calf.

There were hectic days in late spring of 1910, but Martin made progress. He borrowed a scraper from Nick Maerschbecker to use after a thunder shower when the sod was too wet to turn. He had to have a dam for water after the showers stopped, but his oxen were better at pulling the plow in a straight line than going back and forth making a dam. To make an ox change his ways is like trying to hammer a nail into iron. He would have done better hitching his boys to the scraper. He pushed and hit his two oxen, and his temper flared. Fred Martin had pledged himself to the Lord at a revival meeting in Russia, and had the habit of looking toward heaven and calling on "O liever Heiland" for help, but this day he let Satan take over and cursed the oxen in plain German: "ihr verdamte Esel" (you damned asses).

But here came Ludwig over the hill riding his bay mare and finding his brother-in-law crying over block-headed oxen. A twinge of jealousy added to Martin's other woes, and he called out, "Where did you get that horse? Who did you beg it from?" These days Neher had been acting superior to the usually more prosperous Martin, for not only did he have Bossie's milk to drink, but had been better nourished than usual with the kettle-full of grits Frau Bitterman had cooked for him the morning after the thunderstorm. She also had given him an empty Watkins baking powder can, warning him that the can belonged to her and was to be returned. So Neher, on a full stomach, was pleased with himself, but one thing he was not happy about was not having his wife with him: "Die natur verlangt's" (Nature demands it). The baby Ottilia was less than two months old and Mathilda a little over one year. Martin was not very sympathetic to Neher's complaints: "She is better off where she is. Do you want to make her pregnant again?" Neher answered that it was fine for Martin to talk, he already had a good number of children.

Martin realized that either he must buy or borrow a team of broken horses although they would be hard to find so late in the spring. But Neher told him of another Crowley some miles to the north who had horses galore. So the two men rode to the homestead of the Jeremiah Crowley family, a cluster of lumber buildings in a grove of cottonwoods in an agreeable valley with level land for fields. These people looked better off than many homesteaders. The woman greeted Neher and Martin, and in spite of the barriers of language, Neher recognized the word "wait" as meaning they were welcome, for he smelled something good cooking. Johanna Crowley had made extra biscuits, and although she would have preferred that the visitors were Scandinavian or Irish-English, she was glad of any company. The Crowleys' son Jack arrived on horseback for the noon meal, dejected because a heifer had not thrown her calf in time and the calf had died. Jack was in no mood for more Russian immigrants. He recognized the horse that his brother Matt had already given them, and thought now the other one wanted a horse from him. Of course he was right, and Neher managed the deal, explaining that they needed another horse to hitch with the Bay. Jack realized their need, but could not take his eyes off what was happening to the stew. Neher's plate of biscuits was covered with beef gravy, to which he had helped himself, and there was very little left for Jack. Martin too had taken food, but not that much. Jack noticed that Martin had his money sack with him, which put a new light on matters, for money was scarce. Jack was surprised that Martin had any, and a deal for three dollars was struck in the barn for the mare named Bess.

Although it took time and work to break the new horse to harness, slowly but surely Martin's dam took shape. These were hard times not only because necessities for everyday living presented such problems in food, water, and shelter, but also because the two men quarreled so often. Then too, Ludwig sometimes grew desperately homesick for Russia and his family. On the particular Sunday after the horse episode, Neher sat on the stone near his unfinished sod house, eating his brined side pork and bread. He fell to his knees, clutching the stone, and screamed. He was not thinking about his sufferings in the Russo-Japanese war, or of the persecution of the Russian people he knew was going on, he simply was very homesick. He did not really enjoy North Dakota's stony prairie.

And his marriage to Christina by "Koopla," the arranged marriage, was not meeting his expectations. When he had first gone to her home with the marriage broker, they had found her placing raised bread dough in the oven, and four huge loaves of freshly baked bread were already on the table. Ludwig thought that if she could bake, they could eat, and she was attractive to look at as well. Men wanted wives to be like their mothers, but Christina Steinert was not like Julianna Neher, especially in her intellect. Christina came from a progressive dorf, but other than Lutheran religious instruction, she had had little schooling, and could not read or even write her name, unlike her older sister Sophie. This displeased Neher, because in Russia you were somebody if you knew how to read and write. His mother had taught him to write, read, and memorize scripture. At his mother's lap he had learned to pray, for Julianna frequently told her children to thank God for whatever they had to eat. On this particular Sunday Ludwig could not pray; he cried and longed for his mother, but he could neither hear nor feel her. Everything was stone quiet, except for a hawk swooping down to her nest, yet today Ludwig was not moved by prairie wild life.

He filled up on Bossie's milk and started on foot toward the Martins, realizing that it was not good to part as they had on Saturday. Sophie offered him a bowl of soup that he devoured in haste. She noticed he had been crying, and her better nature made her forget her own dissatisfaction. "Go to Christina and your little children," she said to him. On his way across the hills to Jaegers, a rabbit jumped out from her nest behind a sage bush, and Ludwig found a litter of young ones, and thought of his own Mathilda and Ottilia. In Jaeger's summer kitchen all was pretty well, except that Ottilia was a colicky baby and cried except when Christina nursed her. Christina wanted the child "gebraucht," or treated to the spiritual balm that she knew the high Germans did not believe in, but Ludwig already had enough troubles.

Frau Jaeger came every day to the summer kitchen and sometimes more than once a day, especially if there were dumplings left over from her family table, for she knew this poor family needed food worse than her dog Fritz. Mrs. Jaeger was a frugal woman, and domineering in her ways. She knew the Nehers depended on her for food and housing, and she gave Christina so many orders about everything, one wonders how she had confidence to do anything. Today Frau Jaeger was even more high-strung, for she knew why Ludwig had come and she did not want this already bereft young woman to become pregnant again. She ordered Christina to keep the baby sucking to prevent impregnation, and told Ludwig Christina was still in the menses from childbirth and he should abstain ("Du sollst 'fast' haben").

Ludwig left the next morning disheartened. The Jaegers were good people, and Mr. Jaeger, realizing Ludwig needed better food, offered him a rabbit trap. Frau Jaeger gave him carrots and potatoes from her root cellar, and Christina added bread she had baked, much nicer than any bread the German woman could bake. Frau Jaeger put all these supplies into a wooden apple box which would give Ludwig a good place to store food. She also exchanged some of her coarser loaves of bread for Christina's as a fair trade for all she was doing for the Nehers, and Christina felt important for having something the other woman wanted.

Carrying that apple box of supplies was not easy, but was there anything enjoyable in this "donnerwetter" country? Not for Neher these days. He kept thinking about the fertile level fields of Russia and wishing he were back, even though he did not like the Russian government that had no respect for German colonists. A few things were better in Russia, others much worse. His mother's words came to him as he trudged over the stony hills, "Dank Gott wenn du was zu essa hascht" (Thank God if you have something to eat), and "Geh, du, mei grosser sohn, an dei kniee and gev dei herz zum Neiland" (Go, my big son, on your knees and give your heart to the Lord God). The last time he had succumbed to the mercy of God had been during the cruelest of battles while he served in the Russo-Japanese War, when he had seen soldier buddies and rows of German colonists bludgeoned and stabbed with long sharp knives the way you butchered a hog, all to save gun powder. That was when Neher went to his knees to ask God the worth of man. At the final battle between Russia and Japan, he remembered how the crazed Russian general had roared at remaining soldiers, grounded beside dead bodies and pools of blood, some sitting, some lying flat beside their half-dead buddies, screaming in pain. But the screams of soldier Ludwig Neher II were to God. The war ended soon after, Russia lost, and Ludwig and his new friend, Adam Wolf, returned home to Karlstal, sick and tired of the slaughter.

Such were his thoughts as he rested on one of North Dakota's million stones, weighing Russia's oppressive politics against the liberality of the American government giving free land to immigrants. Nevertheless, Ludwig had so many immediate needs. He felt the hopelessness of turning over prairie sod into productive soil when he had nothing to work with and was discouraged at every turn. His mother would tell him to pray, but he knew supplies would not come with prayer. At the moment he felt he had nothing to thank God for, and would have to be self-sufficient as his father had been. He stood up, took up his supply box full of food, and started tramping over the hilly country, knowing that his mother would have said, "Son, you cry. But God will supply. What is there in your box? Food. Then thank God for it." Ludwig was battling between two forces these days.

When he reached Martin's farmyard, he discovered his brother-in-law had hitched up Bay with the young mare Bess. Ludwig was angry because he needed the team, not Martin.

Feuds between the two men came more often these days. "Ich brauch aah aa dam" (I need a dam too) Neher said. While Neher had been visiting his family, Martin had managed to borrow a scraper from Nick Maershbecker. He had led the oxen back, telling his Catholic friend that they liked their old boss better and that they just did not do the trick as he had hoped, and he wanted his two dollars refunded. Martin had tied the oxen to Neher's Bay, and the oxen, surprisingly, followed willingly. Maershbecker was annoyed at having his oxen back, and he pointed out to Martin that it was Sunday, when they should be praying and not doing business. Martin, who had given his heart to the Lord some time before, felt badly, but he was glad to get back his two dollars and be rid of the dumb bovines. Annoyed as Maershbecker was, he nevertheless lent Martin his scraper as well, pitying him, and Martin decided after all that Maershbecker was a good man. And in the days that followed, Nature cooperated: Martin and Neher both got their dams built and Bess turned into a well-broken horse. Bay was a good guide horse. Martin would have liked to own her also, although he knew she was not paid for.

If only he could speak English, Martin thought, he would make an agreement to buy the horse from Matt Crowley. He knew this was an evil idea that had a way of creeping into his thinking in bad times, for he could not play that kind of trick on his brother-in-law. Their lives were bound together, and Martin thought about Neher's family and the even more dire needs there. His conscience bothered him, he knew his desire was against God's will, and he knew he did not keep Sundays holy and had not prayed much recently. He realized that he was becoming unreasonable and harsh. He was half dependent on God, and half thrown on his own ingenuity, as to whether he could make the prairie produce his living. Martin noticed that the potatoes were growing; grain stalks in his few patches of plowed soil were lush; and the garden seeds that Frau Walth had given to Sophie were up and growing nicely in his primitive prairie garden. Soon they would have fresh lettuce and onions. "Vor des sollen mir dankbar sei" (For this we should be thankful). He felt more hopeful.

One early morning in late May Martin took a stroll around the hill and up to the high flat where Nature greeted him with a good feeling. The sun had barely risen and cast a golden glow over hills and valleys. Ample showers had made everything green. Wild flowers were blooming. He picked a bouquet of showy golden peas and added several stalks of blue beardstongue, an attractive bouquet. Perhaps this God-forsaken country held more blessings than one realized. He felt newly hopeful as he presented the fresh wild flowers to his moody wife, and she too showed an early morning exaltation of spirit. She always had been fond of flowers. Martin fetched water from the dam in an empty syrup pail, arranged the flowers in the can, and set them on a flat stone close to the garden. It added color to the whole place, and Martin felt elated.

A Trip to Hebron for Supplies

Surprising what flowers can do. Martin felt happy enough that morning to think of a new idea, that he and Neher ought to hitch up Bay and Bess for a wagon journey into Hebron, where the town was developing sufficiently to have provisions for new settlers and where there were people with interests in religion, both protestant and Catholic. Neher agreed, and pointed out that they had better go soon, for Bay was about to have her colt. Neher and Martin sat in the high wagon seat. They would be back the next evening, Martin told Sophie, who was happy to think that Fred would bring supplies if there was a store in Hebron.

The iron wheels of the wagon rolled slowly across the rutless prairie at dawn on a Tuesday morning, the jangle of the wheels blending with the lush grass. Martin had taken along a sharp knife to cut fresh grass from a slew for horse fodder. On a sudden thud, a front wheel stopped. Neher jumped down and rolled away another one of the million stones. That was the start of a road, when a passing settler moved a stone. As the horses slowed toward the top of a hill, the men could see a vast display of level land, the sort they would have liked to have but had not been given. Martin wanted to talk, in spite of his many quarrels with Neher, who was worse off than he in many ways, but had the advantage of speaking English better. They talked of the many nationalities that were moving in: Irish, Norwegian, Hungarian, German, and mostly "Rooshens" whom everyone laughed at.

At the top of a hill they saw a man guiding a one-share plow with two grays hitched to it. He was breaking up a new patch of prairie, and Neher slowed down the horses. As they drew level to him he called out "Good day." But the man did not much care to stop. He said his name was John Loritz, that he was German, and where did they come from? Neher had to tell him he did not speak High German, but would like to become acquainted, and asked, teasingly, whether he would be willing to part with some of his good land. "Nothing doing," the man said. "Is that all you have to say? I have no time for such nonsense" (Nein, nein, des gibst nicht. Ist das alles was ihr wollen? Ich habe kein zeit fur solke dum-heiten"). Loritz went on his way sulking for having wasted time on another batch of "Rooshens." Neher laughed, but Martin felt badly, knowing that Neher's outspokenness had made for bad feelings between them and this German. Neher hollered after Loritz, did the road lead to Hebron? Loritz shouted back that it did.

Martin and Neher continued southward, passing many established homesteads along the way, most on better land than theirs, they thought. They reached Hebron in the late afternoon, and asked the way to the livery stable from a high-German woman working in her garden who directed them to the stable and well. In her own back yard the men noticed a sow in a pen giving suck to her young. In another pen were chickens spreading their wings in the dust. There were eggs in nests built on the east wall of the chicken coop and a dozing rooster. Martin remarked about what a good start this family had, and the German woman gave hope: "Nur, nur geduld. Das vermehrt sich alles mit der zeit" (Patience, everything grows with time).

Finding the livery stable was easy. Martin was rather nervous, but Neher, as usual, was in a hurry to see what kind of deals he could make with the little bit of money he had. The horses drank at the trough and the men pumped fresh water into their cupped hands and drank. The horses ate the cut slough grass and Neher remarked that he needed a sickle, an English word he had learned from Crowley. The men walked over to the blacksmith shop, where a man busy sharpening plowshares hardly took the time to look at them. Neher tapped him on the shoulder and asked whether he was a German-from-Russia. "Nae, Nae, ich bin ung-gar" (No, I am Hungarian) he said. It took Neher to coax the Hungarian into friendliness and a good business deal. Neher bought a sickle and Martin had his plowshare sharpened. A drayman arrived with his team and a load of blacksmith supplies ready to unload if Koverik could pay cash, and again Martin thought how wealthy a town this seemed and wished he were that far along. Neher told him not to grumble. The two were provoked at each other and continued walking through town, Martin a few steps behind Neher, and they entered a store. Neher grew hungry just thinking about those little fish in the oblong metal cans, but had no money for such luxuries. He bargained for them anyway, leaving the store manager to wonder whether he would ever see his money. Thus Neher enjoyed his second can of sardines, as he had before in Bismarck during the storm. He talked fast and continually, as if the sardines had given him strength.

Next Martin and Neher went to the Schweigert-Ewald Lumber Company. They needed so much they did not know where to begin. Martin bought fence supplies for the garden and paid cash, rather showing off his coins, which the manager was delighted to have. Neher, however, said he could not pay cash, for he had been a poor Russian soldier ("Ich war aa armer Russlander soldat"), and promised Schweigert to do so when he was able. The German was furious, saying he had had to give lumber to a German-Russian to build a coffin for his child, a better reason than Neher's, with whom he had no patience. But finally Schweigert wrote out on a scratchpad that Neher was to pay by fall, at least before winter set in.

The men visited most of Hebron's establishments, buying only what they dearly needed, and then Martin looked around for Neher, but found himself talking to thin air, for Neher had gone to the Northern Pacific depot to see the trains. There was quite a lot of excitement at the Hebron depot on that particular day: the steam-engine was being replenished with water, and quite a number of passengers had debarked. Neher mingled with townspeople and discovered they spoke the same dialect he did.

Some were awaiting the arrival of relatives. One family was waiting for the Phillip Ochsner family, whom Neher had known in Russia.

Most passengers were foreign, persuaded by friends or relatives to come to Dakota to seek land for homesteading, and others had heard that Hebron had a brick manufacturing firm that might employ men. The Ochsner family had been promised housing near the brick yard where Mr. Ochsner could walk to work. Even before their sponsor could greet them, Neher pushed his way forward, but when the newcomers asked whether they could make a living here, Neher could not give his former dorf-friends much encouragement, considering the state he was in—hungry most of the time. He gave Ochsner one pitiful look and began to cry. Ochsner sensed that things were not so rosy for Neher and asked whether he was homesick. He was hoping for some encouragement. But the troubled Neher advised him to stay in town if he could find work, and then he left. He was a man of rapidly changing moods; not even Martin could understand him. One minute he was in a state of elation, the next he cried.

They spent the night in the livery stable sleeping in a stall on the ground. The next day they started the trip home, slowly, for Bay was very pregnant. Martin and Neher had plenty of time to talk about the work that lay ahead of them. Martin had a shanty with a roof and his family with him, whereas Neher's wife and two babies still lived in the Jaegers' summer kitchen. His soddy had acquired a rectangular shape, but was not nearly finished. He spent much time digging out an underground cellar to keep cow's milk and whatever other food he could beg from more settled families, such as Mrs. Bitterman's side pork and bread.

A Homestead Made a Home

Neher jumped off the wagon, telling Martin he would see him the next morning, and crisscrossed pastures and fields on his way to the Jaeger place, where he joined his bereft wife Christina and two babies. The colicky Ottilia (or Odeela) did not need a man's presence; she whimpered almost continually. She clearly was in pain and her parents thought she would die. And Neher too wanted comfort for body and soul and the warmth of a woman. But Christina scolded: hadn't he brought anything from town? They needed so much, especially for the sick child. She wished they had stayed in Russia, where someone could have given her "Gotteswilla braucha," the healing meditation, and the child would have been better soon. Frau Jaeger appeared on the scene, giving her usual stern admonishments. She sent Neher to the house for her husband to give him left-over supper, and Neher filled up on stew of liver, carrots, and dumplings. It didn't taste like his mother's cooking, but his stomach needed food. Neher visited with Herr Jaeger and got good advice, using his outgoing nature to good advantage.

Early the next morning Frau Jaeger called Neher over for a big bowl of barley cereal, then urged him to hurry and get his family out of the summer kitchen so that her family could use it during the summer months. She pointed out that it was not her duty to support Neher's family, and that he had no right to expect such prolonged services. The Germans had not asked the Russo-Germans to come, she said. Neher hung his head, ashamed; for once words failed him. He thought of what his mother would say: be thankful, and let it be known ("Sei dankbar, un lasse sie es wissa"). Regretting what she had said, Frau Jaeger made up a pail full of potatoes, carrots, and beets from the root cellar for Neher to take along, but reminded him to bring back the pail. And Herr Jaeger gave him parting advice, that he had better dig a well, for it might not rain for several months and he would have no water. Neher departed on foot across the prairie, with vigorous steps, almost running, and without seeing it, stepped right into a cactus patch. The painful stickers pierced his worn shoes, and he could not get them all out with his coarse fingers. He went on trying to ignore the pain. Neher approached Martin, firmly asking him to help for a few days to finish the house, and Martin realized that he would have to. Helping out was a must in those days.

The next project at the Neher homestead required much sweat and backbreaking work, and for once Neher had beginner's luck. The well diggers struck water at twenty feet, not the best, but it was water. In their first months on a claim, settlers lugged water from creek holes, ponds, or dams. If you were close to a river or had a natural spring with a steady stream of clear water nearby, you thought yourslf blessed. Always water was a worry, and having it provided security, but one was not to brag, or he might be told "Och, du bra-aler, du hascht besseres wasser, un ich hab bessera spchpeck' (You braggard, you have better water and I have better side pork).

Martin and Neher lined their first wells with prairie stones, and a few years later extended the well with a frame box, and later still a pulley and rope attached to a pail replaced the more dangerous system. This was the famous "wishing" well of song and legend. Hungry children would be told to go to the well and get a cold drink. Often wells were not conveniently near the house, and so a trough was built for watering horses, and near it a hollowed stone used as wash-basin, where one could dunk his head to wash face and hair. The stone also was a good place to sit and think.

Early summer of 1910 was particularly wet for North Dakota, with such a steady flow of thunderstorms saturating the prairies that they appeared a land of limitless prosperity. Little did newcomers realize that the countryside also could become very dry. But this June even sod broke up easily, like moist cake. Their cellars dug, Martin and Neher fitted a floor of 2x4 lumber, most of which Martin had bought because he had more cash. Martin's house was finished first, and Neher was dismayed, but they next went to work on his. A rectangular one-room sod house rose in good order, its top reinforced with a few two-by-fours supported with the trunks of trees.

There had to be some place to cook food and bake bread. Martins had a cast-iron range that their friend Walth had delivered by wagon from Richardton, with which they could bake and make one-dish meals. The garden was good that year, so they had beet and onion tops and dill weed to add to soups of chicken broth or rabbit bones. Nehers built a stone fireplace like the ones in Russian dorfs on the northwest corner of the house, but had not taken into account the northwest winds that would blow smoke into the house. Ludwig had planned in a couple of months also to build a kitchen shack. The climate of South

Russia is milder than North Dakota's, and their first winter here had not been severe in spite of the one February blizzard, so Ludwig did not realize how inadequate his fireplace of gumbo and prairie stone would be. He was in a hurry to make the house habitable so he could bring Christina and the two babies to live there and out of the Jaegers' kitchen.

Arranging to move the family proved difficult. The Bay had had her colt and would not leave it, so Neher needed another horse. He went to the Jeremiah Crowley ranch, even though he knew that most of their horses had not yet been broken to harness. Neher engaged in a complicated hand-waving conversation with John Crowley before he could make him understand what he wanted. Crowley had taken over the responsibility for his ranch, the first on this part of the Knife River, because his father Jeremiah had drowned and his older brother Matt had moved to Elm Creek. John (whose name by now had become Jack) was left to manage the ranch with his mother and sisters, and on this particular morning, was eager to get on with his work. He was tempted to ride away and leave Neher standing there. Crowley was getting impatient, but just as he reached for his pony to ride away, Neher touched one of the horses, and Crowley understood: it was a horse the man wanted, and it was quickly settled that Neher might borrow one.

So it was that Pacer teamed with Martin's Bess to pull the wagon to the Jaeger's place. The horses' hooves cut deep into the road, for there had been another downpour the night before. Martin went along, sensing trouble, for the horses were not used to being hitched together. All went well until they neared the Jaeger place, when Pacer refused to go farther and vaulted into the air. Herr Jaeger witnessed the scene from his yard and thought he could help by bringing out his tamer team, guessing that Neher was coming after his family. He asked his wife to cook up a soup and send along a supply of carrots, potatoes and anything she could spare for those poor people. Mrs. Jaeger was glad to agree this time, for she too had compassion for the Neher family.

What belongings the Nehers had were packed into Jaegers' wagon: "Danke, danke, danke, ihr sen herz-gute leit" (Thank you, thank you, you are good-hearted people). In spite of Frau Jaeger's commanding ways and her wanting the Nehers out of her summer kitchen, she regretted their leaving and felt deep pity. The summer kitchen now was empty of the family that she so proudly had looked after and provided with food from her root cellar. She realized too that this Russian woman could do some things better than she, but she could not let her know it. Frau Jaeger had a deep concern for those Neher babies, and she advised Neher one more time, as he left, to watch out lest he get his wife pregnant too soon again. At the last minute she rushed into her house to fetch a clean folded flannel blanket and a couple of her husband's mended shirts which, out of her over-flowing heart, she gave to this very poor family. She begged Neher to change his shirt, his own would rot soon, for he was a man who sweated much. He could perfectly well have washed his shirt; it looked like a gunny sack dragged over a gumbo patch—but a man was not to be seen without a shirt, and besides, washing was woman's work.

Herr Jaeger hitched his team of trusted gray mares to a wagon that carried everything the Neher family owned. Christina knew that she was leaving a place where there had been shelter, safety, and bread and milk for her babies and herself, and that now she was going to a life that would resemble even less her comfortable dorf life and was not even as certain as the lot of her sister Sophie. Outspoken as Frau Jaeger could be, she was helpful and good. Now Christina was faced with staying alive without money, with no garden, and not much of anything. No wonder her face showed strain as she said her thank-yous and good-byes.

Herr Jaeger led the way along the twin wheel tracks meandering toward the northeast, rather relishing the honor of bringing this mother and her babies home. Neher and Martin followed with their wagon and less well-broken team, Bess and Pacer. By following the head wagon, the horses were less likely to tangle and run away, even though Pacer reared up at the sound of strange voices. Neher and Martin had not properly understood Pacer's name. They heard what sounded like "Baezer," (for Sweeper) and called him that. Martin had it in mind to buy Baezer from Crowley if he'd settle for not too many of his dwindling dollars, thinking Bess and Baezer would make a good team. But when he let Neher in on the idea, Neher complained again that he was the one who had made preliminary negotiations, and that Martin was reaping the benefits while he had nothing, once more angry that he was poor and never keeping up with Martin. Neher even claimed that Martin had been able to continue making money while he, Neher, had had to serve in the Japanese war; it wasn't right. Martin only smirked.

The days that followed were hard. Nehers lived in no more than a squat on the prairie, little fit for babies. Odeela was colicky and screamed all night, and Dilda followed suit. Frau Bitterman smeared their bellies and excercised their arms and legs, praying, and the babies fell asleep. She made camomile tea for the children to drink, and it was fortunate that there were such good women to doctor, relying on remedies handed down from generation to generation. There was no better way.

Nor were there furnishings to move into the sod house, except for the sagging spring bed that Jaegers had reluctantly given up. But any bed at all was a luxury, and Neher was proud he could provide it, until, as he joked, he could sleep in a king's bed. More usual was a mat of straw placed on the board floor or on the ground. The Jaegers also had given Nehers several sectional wood boxes to store the few dishes and blankets and the rags used for diapering and wrapping the babies. The boxes could also hold the family's few articles of clothing, since they did not have enough for a complete change for each person.

They were fortunate in having some sunny days, which made work easier. Christina realized she needed a pile of dry wood for a cooking fire, and gathered up twig sheddings and dry remains of last year's growth along the creek, piling the fuel into a corner of the house. The bed was in the northeast corner, the straw bed for children at the southeast corner, the south wall was fitted with two small windows (truly a refinement that made this more than an elaborate coyote hole), and firewood was at the southwest corner. The northwest corner resembled a Russian hut and was where a stove and chimney would go. On the west wall near the wood pile was a door, then a few steps in, a cellar door fitted on to a square two-by-four foundation and some flooring. Under that was the cellar dugout serving as refrigerator. The rest of the floor was ground, with Jaeger's gunny sacks as scatter-rugs. Christina eyed the situation with disdain, resolved at least to give the earth floor a clay smear, as people did in Russia.

Christina's Works and Days

Christina's first days on the homestead were hectic. Among many other things, she needed water for drinking and cooking. Ludwig had told her about the new well that gave water steadily. There was plenty of it, but using it for drinking and cooking was something else. Christina did not find it tasted as good as the water at Jaegers'. Ludwig had been drinking from the well, but not steadily and had suffered no ill effects. But Odeela developed diarrhea, and there was nothing like toilet paper or changes of clothing to take care of her. Frau Bitterman was summoned. She said there was too much salt, potash, and soda in the water, and told Christina to take clear water from a creek hole and boil it for camomile tea. Elizabeth Boehler, who lived not far away, grew a lot of camomile in her garden, Frau Bitterman said.

Christina was glad that there were a few older women living nearby even if she did not have the security of Russian dorf life, where older people lived among the young, and where grandmothers had the last word as long as a man was not around. Christina needed help, for she was afraid. The Nehers had a barrel and two pails they had borrowed from Martin for water, and it was Christina's job to keep these filled so that the staves would not shrink from the rims and the barrel go to pieces. She needed clear good-tasting water to cook with and to make camomile tea. Over the hill to the south she found a natural spring that had formed a pool of clear water (except for water insects on the top). She scooped water out with the dipper she had brought from Russia, then tied a cloth over the pail to strain out the water life. Then she had to lug the two pails full of water over the hill. Little Dilda ran along close by, rubbing her eyes, crying from the mosquitoes, and wanting her mother to carry her. Christina could not very well carry both pails of water and the fifteen-month-old as well. So she sat Dilda on her shoulders, expecting the child to hold on. But she had scarcely hoisted the two pails and taken a few steps when Dilda let go and began falling. Quickly Christina dropped one pail of water and grasped the frightened child. It took a long time to reach home and a lot of water had been lost, but Christina was glad to have what was left.

Meanwhile Ludwig had reached the sod house first, to find Odeela exhausted from crying. He picked her up, and for the moment realized that he had another child, his daughter, a girl baby again. He had not yet had a chance to get to know his second child. In Russia it was considered shameful for a woman to present her man with girl babies. The first-born, let alone the second, should have been a son. But today Ludwig pressed against his chest this infant who needed tender attention and he felt strange compassion for the little life he and Christina were responsible for. He wondered whether Christina had enough strength both to nurse the child and to carry water. Ludwig thought of his own mother, how much she had suffered from lack of food, as she grew up in a pastor's home where almost everything was shared and given to wayfarers, denying the family. He remembered his mother always wanting to make a living off the land. Now she knew, from his letter, that he, her oldest son, owned land.

Ludwig was glad that his mother did not really know how desperate their needs were out on that hilly prairie. He wished his mother could cuddle baby Odeela as she had Dilda, and feed her gruel. Ludwig hardly knew the woman he married, realizing only that she was inwardly disturbed most of the time and talked to herself in low tones and abrupt screams. She was not at all like his own mother, wise and confident in spite of hardships. Christina always was in a state of fear, especially today. Ludwig scolded her, frightening her even more. She had had enough of hauling water and now had to nurse the baby and her breasts were limp. There was hardly anything to cook, and everyone was hungry, but Mrs. Jaeger had sent beets along, Ludwig pointed out, and they could build a fire and throw in side pork. It would smell good.

Nature cooperated with the Nehers on their first few days together in the homestead. Ludwig got the outdoor fire going. They made a stew in the cast-iron kettle with Frau Jaeger's garden stuff, good creek water, and pieces of fat pork. But Christina wondered what they would eat when the Jaeger food was used up, and she expected the worst. There were other neighbors around, she thought, who would have to help them out, and perhaps Ludwig could catch a young rabbit. But there was not time enough to worry. While the sun shone, there was hay to make for winter feed for stock. But the two babies wailed most of the time, probably because they did not have enough to eat and were uncomfortable in their itchy clothing. Christina was not prepared for living on the prairie alone, so unlike what she had known in the Russian dorf. She had two babies and a man she scarcely knew, and she felt, all in all, thrust into chaos.

It was time to cut winter hay from the lush stand of oats that had been sowed on the plowed patch of land in the spring. Ludwig cut it with his scythe, a hot and exhausting job, for which he was glad to have fresh well water near at hand to drink. Then he picked up the oats with a pitchfork and carried them to make a pile in the yard, hoping it would not rain before the oats dried. But that night there was a thunderstorm, stronger than usual. He arose at daybreak to see how much damage had been done, and thought things looked pretty bad.

Ludwig was not in the habit of calling on God, either to thank or to petition Him, at least not as he should have. He thought he was self-sufficient, and although he did not completely reject the thought of God the Helper, he did neglect to place Him first. Instead, when conditions became unbearable, he stretched his arms to the eastern horizon and called on his mother, using her familiar words: "Take the Lord into your heart and let Him strengthen and lead you" (Nimn den Heiland in dei herz un laz Ihn dich staercha un fuehra). But Ludwig could not comprehend her words and resigned himself to negative thoughts. His crop was gone, he thought, as he walked back into the soddie to tell Christina.

But he said nothing, for in the house the child was screaming again, and he realized Christina had enough of a burden trying to quiet down her two babies. Odeela needed to be "braucht," so Ludwig started walking to the homestead of George and Elizabeth Boehler. He knew he could not ask them for food, for they also were as poor. But Mother Boehler would be good all around, especially for moral support, for she was extraordinarily patient.

Mother Boehler was an amiable person, and managed to produce something to eat. Vater George tended to be idle, usually saying he could do something tomorrow but not today. But Elizabeth Boehler had chosen a garden spot with dark fertile soil and her last year's plantings had produced much. They had dug a root cellar and lined it with prairie stones, and preserved root vegetables very well in the even, cool temperature. Her herb patch had plants for many uses: medicine, perfume, and insect repellent. On this particular day, Ludwig arrived so early he had to wake her, but she made a fire in the stove to boil water for an herb tea and for breakfast coffee and oatmeal. She did not mind being disturbed, for she knew she was needed, and sent Ludwig to the cellar for potatoes to bake in the oven while it was hot. Again, Ludwig wished that his household were that far along.

Throughout those first crucial years, Mother Boehler was a great help to the Nehers, a moral support for Christina and tender toward the little girls. She shared a corner of her root cellar, and pickled watermelons and cucumbers in a small barrel for the Nehers as well. Fortunately her garden produced heavily in 1909 and 1910 and her root cellar was filled amply. Gardens were her specialty, and she would talk out loud to vegetables, encouraging watermelons and pumpkins to grow fast, and she was an expert with herbs, knowing just which ones were mild for children, and which stronger for older people. She felt called on to help others. But she also had troubles. The Boehlers needed more farm implements in order to plant barley and wheat. George Boehler suffered from chronic fatigue that herbs did not cure. He was always tired and wanting to sit on the shady side of the sod house. He breathed hard, especially when there was work to do: "Mother I don't know, but I can't do it, you get around much better" (Mutter, ich waez, aver ich kanz net dura; du kantscht baesser rum kumma).

Having Mutter Boehler as her closest neighbor made Christina feel secure. She was more open with her than with anyone else in expressing her feelings, and less intimidated by her than by Frau Jaeger. She appreciated all that Jaegers had done for her, and she wished she could be like the high Germans, but always felt inferior. Christina was a submissive person, but when she was with Mutter Boehler, life in those hills became more endurable even though it was never like the dorf where everyone minded everyone else's business. She grew to love Mutter Boehler, who encouraged her and gave her credit for what she did.

On that day after the thunderstorm Christina had been trying to get the fire started in the fireplace on the northwest corner, when the wind blew grassy smoke into the house. Dilda coughed and cried, and Christina took her outdoors. When Ludwig and Mutter Boehler arrived Odeela had stopped whimpering, but Mrs. Boehler, noticing how pale she was, brought her outdoors for air and revived her. However, not everything turned out badly from that night and morning. The thunderstorm that had leveled oats and wheat turned out less harmful than Ludwig feared, for the wheat rose again and the oats straightened enough to be cut with a scythe. Mutter Boehler stayed with Christina and the babies for most of the day. She had brought some cooked vegetables with her, and Christina's spirits lightened. She loved to cook and bake bread, but sometimes, as today, she was baffled and frightened by living on the open prairie. When Mutter Boehler was around, however, she felt secure and confident. Between the two, they got the fire started, and Christina mixed a bit of lard, and a little flour and some onion slices, added water, and brought it to a boil for a thickened broth that Frau Jaeger called flour soup. This time Mutter Boehler added some of the chopped vegetables, dill, onion and beet tops. The result was a mixture of high and low German soups, or so Ludwig called it. It was good. Mutter Boehler discovered that Christina had a knack of making something to eat out of almost nothing, and she took a dipperful home to her ailing husband.

Mining and Harvesting

Everyone told Ludwig to spend June and July getting fuel ready for the winter. But there were so many other things that needed attention, and he had no equipment to scrape coal from the ground. As usual, Ludwig began with a visit to Matt Crowley, who he found had just made a large beef stew, and aggravated as he was by the visit, Matt dipped out beef and potatoes which Ludwig ate hungrily. The poor sucker had needs, Crowley assumed by the way he was flinging about his arms. Crowley left the room for a few minutes, which Ludwig used to help himself to a little more stew. He was surprised to notice the lingering coal fire in the cast-iron stove. Crowley's hired man explained in German that once dried, the coal could be placed on top of a wood fire, and if there was not too much soil mixed with the coal, it made a long-holding fire. Crowley added that there might be a vein of coal on Neher's land, and Ludwig became so excited he wanted the men to come with him right away to show him.

Matt Crowley was annoyed by such demands, but was compassionate enough to know that Neher needed help this first year on the prairie. Crowley himself already had experienced a number of harsh winters, so he had his cowhand hitch up a team to the grass mower while he got pick and shovel. He tied the tools with a rope onto the mower, heaved himself onto the seat, grabbed the harness lines and giddy-apped the horses toward the west, leaving Neher to follow on foot the way a colt does a mare. Neher jumped about like a jackrabbit, braying with laughter, the happiest man in Mercer County at the thought of all the machinery and tools this Irishman was willing to bring him to help out. Matt was a man of few words and great actions.

On this visit, Matt met Christina and the two little ones for the first time, and noticed the bare circumstances under which this poor shy woman had to carry on, the family's actual destitution. He caressed Dilda, running his fingers through her hair and set her on his knee as he squatted on the ground, the rancher's usual position for accommodating a cup of coffee. Dilda loved the attention, chattering away in German baby-talk. She guided the friendly stranger indoors to see her baby sister Odeela lying in a wooden box lined with a straw-filled mattress. She had a little pillow Frau Jaeger had made with fine feathers of prairie chickens. Matt Crowley was touched by the sight of these children. The baby was tightly wrapped in swaddling clothes and sucking on its fist. He reached for the baby's other hand when Dilda pulled it out of the tight wrappings. He opened the tiny fingers and wrapped them around his forefinger, feeling their softness. He was moved by the pathetic one-room house and the family's struggle to survive, and he was not sorry to have taken time to try to help. Although Matt Crowley could neither speak to nor understand Mrs. Neher, he showed her that he admired her, for she was a good looking woman. But Christina was ill at ease, and wished that she had some of her good sweet bread to serve with coffee as she would have done in Russia.

Matt Crowley and Ludwig Neher hiked over the hill to the southeast carrying pick and shovel. On the side of a coulee, Matt noticed in the cut-off, layers of dark and light. He dug until his blade hit a hard pan, and was surprised to find that he had hit a layer of coal. Neher had not known what coal was until he came to America, when he had seen its benefits in the heated stove in Bismarck during the blizzard. And now to be discovering layers of grayish black coal shales on his own land was to him unbelievable. He dug away, and Matt began to realize that Neher was not a parasite but a hard worker.

The days that followed were ones of hard toil for both Ludwig and Christina, raking, digging, lugging. The oat hay had to be hand raked and carried to a stack with a pitchfork which Neher had borrowed from Crowley. And Christina worked right along with Ludwig, for girls in Russia were trained to work even harder than men. Picking and digging coal shales Ludwig found was the hardest work of all, but he seemed not to mind. for coal promised to be so great a blessing. The pile grew through July against the windowless side of the sod house.

Matt Crowley knew that when his wheat was ready for cutting, Neher's would be too, for they had been planted at the same time. He owned a grass mower but not yet a header. Matt threw his hat into the waving grain, and as it settled on top and rode there, he knew it was time to cut. He looked toward a red sunset and recited:

> Evening red and morning gray,
> Sends the rancher on his way.
> Evening gray and morning red,
> Brings some rain upon his head.

Sure enough, sunrise the next morning showed gray clouds with golden rims, and Matt was happy. The signs were sure and right, and the beautiful golden grain soon lay in orderly rows. He asked his hired man to harness up another team of horses and traveled to the Nehers, where Christina greeted him warmly for being so good a person. She assumed he could understand her gratitude, if not her words. Matt walked over to the house to look at the children. Odeela sucked on his finger and Dilda pulled on his pants. He had nothing to give them except affection and pity, thinking that next time he would carve a toy for them to play with.

Ludwig was impressed by America's labor-saving machinery. The way Crowley's grass mower stripped his wheat field was a miracle, a wonderful happening that he had not expected. Once the grain lay in rows, heads up and straw down, it was time to make sheaves and bring them in, and Christina would have to work with him, as well as take care of home and children.

Christina showed Ludwig how to prepare the threshing floor, the way she had done it in Russia, and the same way as it had been done in Biblical times. Ludwig was reluctant to listen to, let alone accept, a woman's advice, but this time Christina's word ruled. He did not want to admit that she knew more than he, and he let his thoughts wander to memories of his youth. He himself had never had much training in actual farming methods in Russia. He had cared for hogs and other stock, helping his father on the Count's resort and orchard and garden in Karlstal. This time Christina was the one with the proper skills.

First she selected a gumbo plot part way up the hill and made the spot round, clearing it of sagebrush and prairie grass. She lugged water up the hill from the dam and poured it onto the plot, then added dry grass and leaves and tramped the sticky mud down with horse hoofs, guiding Bay round and round on a halter, her colt scampering in and out of the confusion to snatch sucks of milk. Then this firm and solid threshing floor had to be smoothed out, which Christina did with a stone resembling a spatula. In spite of such hard work, Christina felt exhilarated because she was able to teach her man something, and because she could see that the same thing might be done to the floor of the sod house to get rid of troublesome ants that were crawling about. Sure enough, when the bedroom floor was treated as well, their home looked less like a coyote hole. At the end of these exhausting days, the children were crying for attention. Christina had placed the baby's crib box on the shady side of the hay stack while the floor was drying. To quench their thirst, Christina kept a gallon of sour milk handy, to be drunk like water. Ludwig was not too fond of this warm sour milk, remembering the cool milk his mother made him drink, and now he followed a dipper-full of clabber with a mouthful of wheat to get rid of the sour milk taste.

It was remarkable how well the threshing floor turned out. A quick thunderstorm passed over the Neher homestead, just enough to give the floor a second treatment, and although it flattened rows of wheat and made Ludwig and Christina more tense than ever, it also quickened the ripening of the grain. Tortured days followed. Christina carried armsful of wheat down the hill to the threshing platform. Not wanting to wear out her only pair of shoes, she tied rags around her bare feet to protect them from cactus stickers. Ludwig borrowed a sledge hammer to beat out the wheat, then Christina carried armsful of straw into the yard, for if even a few heads of grain remained, they would be good for the cow. They had prepared a site for a round strawstack the night before at some distance from the haystack, so that if one burned, the other would not catch fire. Ludwig was beginning to learn about precarious North Dakota weather, that lightning could strike and start fires. Christina called on God to preserve their crop, for they needed every grain. Ludwig thought her behavior odd, although he remembered his mother also praying out loud, but that was different. He thought Christina weak, for he did not himself think that he needed God that badly. Christina sensed his mockery and had the nerve to tell him that he ought to become a convert. In Russia Christina had been to a revival meeting at her Lutheran Evengelical Church, calling on her loving Saviour to redeem her from sin and promising to take Him into her heart. That is why she talked out loud as though God were right beside her, and often cried as well when she was very tired or when Ludwig made sarcastic remarks about her praying.

Odeela cried a lot and Frau Bitterman again was summoned. But instead of removing the band around the baby's abdomen covering her navel, she tightened it, and despite the heat, wrapped the child even more, in the belief that air, whether in summer or winter, caused illness. She was only acting according to what had been passed down to her from elder-women in the old country. She performed "brauching," rubbing with vinegar and fat, moving the baby's arms and legs in rhythmic motions while she said a holy meditation. Then she wrapped Odeela in more coverings and said she would fall asleep. But she did not, and her crying turned to whimpers and her breathing to spasms. The parents became truly alarmed that she would die, and resolved to take her to Frau Jaeger, dismissing Frau Bitterman to walk home alone dejectedly and wondering what she had done wrong.

Carrying their two children, Ludwig and Christina walked quickly to the Martin place to borrow the team of horses and wagon to drive to the Jaegers. Without thinking, Christina loosened the navel band and other wrappings, giving the baby more air. It was the right thing to do, even though it violated old wives' practices. As soon as Mrs. Jaeger saw her, she knew from the fever and gasping that the baby's lungs were infected. She placed a heated bag of oats in a woolen sock on the baby's chest, replacing it with another when it cooled. She bathed the infant in cool vinegar water to cut the fever, and in a few hours Odeela fell asleep, having been fed an oatmeal "brei" or pap. Mrs. Jaeger felt a special attachment to Odeela, for after all she had delivered her, and the infant had been named after Mrs. Jaeger's own daughter Ottilia. Once again Mrs. Jaeger felt the plight of the Neher family and gathered up a few more items for Christina to take back with her. She gave them an extra bottle for the baby, first pouring in a handful of sand, adding water, and giving it a good shake, so that the sand would scour the bottle clean.

It had not occurred to Christina, when she married the dashing soldier, that her childbearing years would be spent in such poverty. Her parents had been well off, and her dowry was good enough, but the money she had inherited had been used for travel costs of immigration, and Ludwig had not received soldiers' benefits from the Russo-Japanese War.

August: Threshing

The harvest of late summer 1910 gradually came to an end. The good samaritan, rancher Matt Crowley, appeared quite unexpectedly with his horse-drawn rake, intending to put the rows of grain into suitable piles before it got too ripe. In Russia, after grain was scythed, it was gathered and bound together into sheaves, then carried to the threshing floor to ripen until loose in the husk. Rain and dew were most unwelcome during harvest, so hot weather brought hard work to women, men, children, and animals, for everyone had to work to save every grain possible. Ludwig noticed wheat kernels scattered about on the parched earth in one gumbo patch of his field, and he made it clear the grains would have to be picked up before the crows got them. He had been warned of this bird by Mr. Jaeger but had never seen it in Russia. Everyone except the baby, including Dilda, helped gather grains. Christina rinsed the kernels, soaked them in water, and served them for lunch the next day.

Every time Ludwig picked up the pitchfork that he had bought on time at his last visit to Hebron, he thought of how fortunate he was to be able to use something that handy, and how lucky he was that the lumberman trusted him until fall. Christina had to use her open arms and ten forked fingers to grasp armsfull of ripened wheat and carry them to the gumbo floor. Then to rest herself she led Bay round and round to stamp out as much of the wheat as possible. Then Ludwig would take grain ears and stalks to another stack, and they would sweep wheat and chaff into gunny sacks, the sacks and broom also having been placed on charge lists of Hebron businesses.

The overturned virgin soil on the high flat had produced well. Kernels were large. Ludwig carried a few sacks into the house to keep them dry from rain and dew, and others he placed in a hole at the side of the strawstack for protection. The days became dreary successions of backbreaking work, and during the windiest days, all other work ceased. One at a time, sacks of chaff and grain were carried up to the threshing floor, where the chaff was blown from the grain. Christina threw handful after handful slowly into the air, and the wind blew the chaff away. After winnowing, it was a great pleasure to dip the clean wheat into a special sack, ready to be sold and milled into flour, the staff of life for the Neher family.

Although Christina did not complain of her extreme fatigue and sore back, one evening she developed convulsions, and Ludwig did not know which way to turn. Both babies were screaming. He went to the Boehler homestead for help. (He did not dare ask Mrs. Bitterman, for she still felt let down over her unsuccessful cure for Odeela.) But good Elizabeth Boehler was willing to walk all that way in the night, declaring that Christina was being killed with work, that it was not human anymore, and that she was to stay in bed until she got back her strength.

Nehers felt they were at the mercy of their neighbors, as well as of Hebron merchants, and it was no wonder that Christina had been brought to a state of complete exhaustion by her ox-like labors, malnutrition, and worries about her little ones. She also was homesick, and it comforted her to have Mrs. Boehler around, for she did not understand the man she had married. The arranged marriage had allowed her only ten days' acquaintance before holy matrimony, and then she had come to these wild prairie lands that she knew no better than she did Ludwig's personality. And then she found herself with two babies and hardly anything to sustain them. Ludwig understood little more about her, only assuming that it was up to her to submit to him ("Sie muz dem mann undertan sei"). Nevertheless, Christina knew that she had had more farming experience than her husband, even though his pride kept him from giving her credit for her skill.

Ludwig too was homesick. He had word that his father had died, and wondered about his dear mother's welfare. Nothing made him give way so readily to tears as the mention of the word "mother," for thinking of her brought tender memories and homesickness for Russia herself. After all, there were many good things about Russia, some better than what he found in America. He remembered that his forebears had gradually improved their lives on those steppes, and here he was, again struggling on open prairies, hoping for prosperity and enduring as his forebears had.

"Wie kennen mir a leva macha; unz gehts grad wie alle meine vor-eltera ganga isch" (How can we make a living here; we're getting just what our forebears got). Ludwig recalled the time his father was assigned the worst of Russia's silty, clay land, where they could not raise enough wheat to chew on, and now here in America he had only hills and stones for his allotment. "Des isch net so schlimm. Mir hen doch die hoeh womer a gute ernt griegt hen" (It is not that bad. We have the high flats that have given us a nice harvest this year). That is what Martin said to his disappointed brother-in-law, who retorted, "Du bischt a-a net immer so Gnad-reich" (You are not always that praiseworthy either).

It was late August 1910. Nature cooperated with spasmodic heat waves. With the limited number of threshing rigs available, everything worked fast. When threshing was completed at the Maerschbecker and Jaeger farms, the rig could be moved to where the greatest need existed among new homesteaders, naturally among the Martin and Neher families. The biggest problem facing the outfit movers was lack of a roadway. Stony hills and rutty vales made it difficult to move heavy equipment to the Martin and Neher homesteads. Martin and Neher drove to the Jaegers with a team and wagon to figure out a safer route than following the winding roadway. They thought the massive wide iron-rimmed wheels of the steam engine could hold out against the hillsides, but there was danger that the threshing machine would tip over.

Watching the steam engine crawl around the prairie hills, people were amazed to think that this massive threshing machine could move without being pulled by humans or animals, and the sight almost made them forget other agonies of this hilly country. But for Maerschbecker and Jaeger the move was all too slow, and their trying to hurry resulted in an accident, the machine turning over in the ruts. Hectic hours followed. Jack Crowley came riding across the hills, having noticed smoke rising, but his advice was ignored as he tried to make himself heard, for the Germans did not understand him. Time was passing, and Crowley shouted louder: "Why the hell don't you use your bunch of kids for power? There are enough of them to give a lift." Nick Maerschbecker heard him and made Martin understand. He called in his boys. Then with an iron lever men and boys set the threshing machine upright and the steam engine pulled it out of the rut. Power came from steam made by burning last year's straw mixed with reeds and weeds, a mystery to Martin and Neher, who in Russia were used only to animal or human power.

Christina and the two little ones had joined the Martin family during the absence of the men-folk. There was great excitement in the Martin yard when the big black monster puffed its way toward the homestead. The few head of stock and the young dog

"Hund" ran around in terror. Children cried and Sophie and Christina rushed about anxiously, not knowing what to think when they saw the roaring, smoking snorter. The lively young Martin boys scampered about. Fred Martin had walked at a fast pace ahead of the machine. He felt hunger pangs as never before and he also knew that everybody else was hungry. Then he remembered that when he had left for the Maerschbecker homestead Sophie had been displeased when he told her that Ludwig was going with him and he did not know when he'd be back. She had complained about having to feed and look after children while he went around to eat at other people's houses, and he had answered quickly that Christina would be coming over and the two could bake some good bread. Approaching now, he met the two sisters cautiously. He teased them for being scared. Fred smelled bread baking. "Aver des schm-acht so gu-et. Sener noch alle em-le-ava?" (How good it smells. Are you still all alive?). "Ja, ja, was sonscht?" (Yes, yes, what else?).

Well, there was bread. Christina had done wonders, letting the dough rise again and again after punching it down, and placing loaves in large well-greased bread pans. All Christina needed, besides the everlasting yeast that Frau Boehler had given her, was a couple of handsful of sugar, some salt, a bit of warm lard, and good milled flour, and she turned out eight massive loaves of golden brown bread. She gave credit for the well-risen bread to Sophie's wonderful cast-iron stove with its large oven. "Du wa-aischt gar-net wie glicklich du bischt" (You do not know how fortunate you are). By comparison, Christina felt all the more her own family's shortages.

The same afternoon, as the threshing rig was moved into the Marin yard, Christina was in a happy frame of mind watching Jaeger, Maerschbecker, and Crowley eat with great appetite the bread she had baked. It was the first time Jack Crowley had stopped at the Martin homestead, and he joined right in eating the bread with the rest of the hungry crew. No one worried about being polite, but ate one piece of bread after another, soon leaving few loaves, which meant that yeast would have to be set again that night and another batch of bread baked the next day. On this afternoon no one mentioned saying grace, whether from the excitement of the puffing engine or the novelty of the mix of nationalities: a high German, a Catholic, and an Irishman, all in the home of a lowly "Russlander." At any rate, Chrisitna was exhuberantly demonstrative. Jaeger had known that Christina could bake the best bread, but Crowley said he had never tasted the like of such bread. His own mother doted on biscuits and flapjacks, but Christina's bread was something else.

Scriptural directives to "multiply" too often were the excuse to ignore common sense in birth control. Some who followed Biblical pronouncements literally thought there was nothing wrong with a surplus of children and were convinced that God will provide and that other people would help out families with many children and many needs. Every household had to be ready to feed a distressed neighbor who brought his throng of kids. If they were God's select, bread had to be dealt out and shared. Homesteaders expected to feed the hungry and share tools, horses, and shelter whenever they could.

Indentured Children

There was a man who had settled earlier in the Golden Valley country to the north and wanted to buy an extra team of unbroken geldings. He made his way to the Knife River horse ranch of Jeremiah Crowley. He too was German-from-Russia with little knowledge of English, but he and the Irishman Crowley made each other understood enough to carry out a horse trade. The man had not threshed yet, and the moon showed signs of a change in the weather. Jeremiah's son Jack, who especially loathed the idea of so many Russo-Germans settling near his ranch, said in his ridiculing manner, "There, way down on the south side of the first long hill another Rooshen has settled with a bunch of kids. You might get a couple of them if you buy them each a pair of shoes. I noticed they are barefoot."

So the Golden Valley homesteader made his way to the Martin homestead and guided his team into the Martin yard. The young dog barked fiercely, reminded of the frightening noises of the threshing rig. The stranger halted his team of gray geldings. Wiping sweat from his forehead with the back of his hand and then his shirt sleeve, Martin was glad to welcome him. Martin had been laying out foundations for a shelter for the few head of stock he owned. Magdalena and the boys were carrying stones from the hillsides, and Martin selected from their pile each stone to make a proper fit for the foundation. After a little small talk, Martin realized that this stranger was also a homesteader and like himself a Russian-German immigrant to America. The man pointed out that while Martin had more than enough children to get his work done, he needed two because he was not yet through with his threshing, and would Martin give him a pair? This cunning dealer had come at just the right time, for Martin had grown impatient with his children, and right on the spot, without even consulting Sophie, he hired out Magdalena and John. His word was command.

Packing the children's clothes was no problem, for they had little more than what they wore, and both were barefoot, good enough reason for a quick agreement and a resolution on the employer's part to buy them each a pair of shoes for winter when he sold his wheat. Quickly Magdalena and John found themselves in the stranger's wagon, with hardly a decent goodbye and rather frightened to be leaving their brothers so suddenly. Sophie was highly perturbed to think that her oldest children were taken away and gone she knew not where, and she gave way to scolding: "Noch net a-mol do-ot-mer waz saga, so gscheid sin sie. Wel-ar- a-a mann isch" (Not telling me anything. He thinks he is so smart, just because he is the man).

The weeks that followed were a terrible ordeal for the two Martin children. The work was treacherous and far too hard. For Magdalena it was never-ending; milking one cow after another tortured her because her hands were weak. At her own home she worked steadily, but also had chances to sit on the shady side of the house and dream a bit about her beloved grandparents so far away who had caressed her when she was a little girl. Now there was no such thing as a gentle human touch. Yesterday she had been a small girl, and today expected to take on adult responsibilities. She often screamed at this crude man who only told her to hurry up, there was much work to be done before bedtime. And the homesteader's wife was no better, an obstinate and filthy woman, in a mulish way always ready for an argument. Most of her energy went to angry outbursts, swinging her arms and screeching that Magdalena and John would not get their new shoes if they did not show more will to work. Nights were the worst times for the Martin children, for, when they ought to have been getting much needed rest, they were plagued with bedbugs. The house was foul with dirt, a perfect place for bedbugs to thrive. Magdalena remembered the bedbugs on board ship, and how upset her mother had been, and now she reacted similarly. She was frightened. If she had known the way home, she and her brother would have started right then.

One Saturday evening the slave-driving man threatened to beat John for crying, saying he was not worth having around. That night John got sick. He cried and cried, and Magdalena shed tears as never before. First the bedbugs, and now her brother in such a feverish condition was too much for her. She cried aloud for her parents, and the "pig woman" as she called her told her to be quiet and go to sleep. Magdalena was horrified by these people's filthy dress, house, and yard, and even by their language.

As if by second sight, Sophie had not given her Fred any peace the whole time her children were gone. She nagged and scolded. That Saturday night she had a premonition that something was very wrong with her children, and she said she was going to them if she had to walk. Fred gave in, and early Sunday morning, the disspirited Martins made their way northward with a wagon and team, inquiring along the way for the whereabouts of the family. There was not much conversation between them, for Sophie was greatly troubled about her children.

By Sunday morning John's fever had subsided but he was subdued. He blinked his half-shut swollen eyes and ignored the stern order to eat the grits before him as he sat close to his sister at the table. John spent most of the forenoon sitting by the side of the sod house petting the bedraggled and half-starved dog who craved affection as much as food. The dog let out a low growl when the man and woman left with their team and buggy to a church service, where they would have much to reckon for. Magdalena was scratching her bedbug sores. Suddenly Doby, the dog, perked up his ears, then barked and ran south where there was a wagon approaching on the horizon. John ran to the windmill and climbed it. He started to cry. If it was his parents, it would be for gladness; if it was not, he would cry for grief and homesickness. He saw that it was his father and mother, but, now insulted and angry, he clung to the high windmill, his hands clasped to the shaft. "Ach Gott, kind, komm doch runder" (O God, child, come down), Sophie called out to him as she descended from the wagon, holding out her hands to him, looking up and pleading that she had felt a warning that all was not well with her children.

Sophie wrote a note in German, informing these strange people that they had taken the children home with them. The Martins drove home at a fast pace, Magdalena in the back of the wagon hearing those two dirty people scold and scold, and John between his "baba un mama," feeling their warmth and security. Both Magdalena and John suffered emotionally. They had been torn too soon from their home in Groszliebental, and the harsh conditions of the past year made them grow up too quickly. The homesteader appeared at the Martins some time later to say that he was disappointed in his two hirelings, especially at what he called the evil boy who was not worth anything. There was an argument, but he handed Martin a few dollars which purchased Magdalena and John each a pair of shoes.

Fred Martin realized the wrong he had done his two eldest children. How could he forget, for Sophie reminded him often sternly. But he never apologized, for that would be humiliating. He did allow himself to reminisce. "I grew up a semi-orphan in Russia, for my mother died when I was but a child. My father remarried, and my stepmother tried to get me out of the house. I had to work as early as I can remember. I often think, how cruel she was, for she did not even want me to come home for a visit for fear she would have to share an extra piece of bread. Today as I think of it I realize I was not the only young boy treated that way. Cruelty was part of discipline in those days. I resolved not to treat my own children that way, but thinking and talking is one thing, and living it is another. Living in desperate times makes one desperate toward others, and one makes wrong decisions out of need." Telling this story was as close as Fred Martin ever came to admitting that he had made a mistake to send off his children to this obscure home. But he did not say that he was sorry.

Autumn

Martin was in a temperamental mood those days, knowing that money from his crops would not cover supplies for his family and shelter for the animals. Where could he ask for help? One Sunday his conscience bothered him, an exceptional experience. He remembered how in Russian dorfs Sunday was deemed holy. Here in America other things became more important than taking time for a prayer meeting. But he found himself praying again for help. "Ach lieber Herr Gott, erbarm dich doch un helf unz aus wie Ihr es bis-her geto-od hascht' (O dear Lord have mercy on us and help out as Thou hast always done). He realized it was not God that had forsaken him, it was Martin himself who had neglected to glority Him all through harvest, and he resolved from then on to have a simple Sunday afternoon prayer and Bible reading, with full agreement from Sophie and Christina.

The early fall of 1910 was crowded with jobs to be done before winter set in, for Nehers and Martins did not want to repeat what they had experienced the year before. They did not want again to appear like a coyote who digs a hole in the ground for refuge from cold and makes kills at random. Sophie and the boys gathered smaller watermelons from the productive melon patch and fitted them one by one into a wooden barrel for pickling. But she needed a cellar to store them. Digging a root cellar was the next job, a place to store vegetables, sauerkraut and pickled cucumbers and watermelons, where the temperature would be cool but not freezing. With the pick and only spade, dirt clumps were loosened and carried away in a bucket, back-breaking work. The Martin boys and Magdalena argued over whose turn it was to gather stones from a nearby hill. Fred Martin did the bossing and scraped the hole into a sizeable room. The result was a marvel: walls lined with stone and ladder steps for a slanted descent. One of the boys found a cluster of shale-like stones and took a sample to his father, who praised him, for they fit just right. Children seldom were praised in those days, lest they think too well of themselves.

A period of dry weather helped spare time for the many tasks to get ready for winter. Based on their experiences of the previous winter, Neher and Martin knew, as they said, that no cow could withstand such elements, let alone unprepared settlers. The next project was to erect a shelter for stock. Prairie stones were placed in a staggered fashion and covered with a smear of gumbo clay. Interwoven tree limbs, cemented with straw and clay were fitted over a few rough boards laid crosswise to make a rude canopy. A thick tree branch or tree trunk made the posts, each pounded into holes and connected with more braided branches for a crib for cattle fodder. The men constructed two such cribs, the larger in the Martin yard and a smaller one in Neher's.

The first snow in October of 1910 was followed by a thaw and Chinook wind. Herr Jaeger appeared one day saying such warm weather was called Indian summer, and he began to talk about Indians, telling Nehers that Indians believed that the Spirit of Nature treats people with a sudden turn in the weather to warn them to ready themselves for the coming winter, and that Neher and Martin ought to take note. He warned them also that often at such times a band of Indians might appear, but that they should not be afraid, because all they wanted would be some of their good bread. He left both families rather alarmed at his predictions, but too busy to dwell long on the possibility of such strange intruders.

The weather continued mild through fall, as if to encourage these new settlers. One fine autumn noon, while her children were asleep, Christina took upon herself to hike toward a cluster of trees a little to the southwest of the homestead. She gathered scattered branches in her apron and started back. She saw two riders slowly aiming their ponies toward her house. She dropped the kindling wood and ran in terror, thinking of the safety of herself and her babies, and remembering Jaeger's warning. These were bound to be the strange roamers of the prairies, just as there had been in Russia. Sure enough, two Indians riding bareback appeared at the front door of the sodhouse. Christina forced a small bench against the door jam, for they had no locks. One of the men knocked on the door, and Christina screamed, "Ach liever Gott, ich hav-jo so angscht" (O dear God I am so scared). The other man looked in through the little window, showing his teeth in a big grin and gestured with his hand toward his mouth. That signal Christina understood, remembering what Jaeger said about her bread. She fetched a loaf of freshly baked bread, opened the door only wide enough to hand it out, and shouted to them to go away. But the men only stood there eating the bread.

Then one of the Bitterman boys, who had noticed the two

riders moving along the hill, arrived to see whether they had indeed stopped at Nehers' place, and thought what would that poor Fra Neher do. In his German brogue, Bitterman let out a few harsh words and made a fist, and with his other hand raised his whip ready to strike as the two strangers mounted their horses and set off at a gallop. The Indians never came back again. Although Christina was not sorry for having given them bread, she never quite got over the fright of that experience. It only added one more fear to her many other anxieties, and made her wish all the more that she was back in Russia, the way it used to be when she grew up.

Winter set in and hardships continued. The families had nothing to read but the Bible and a few hymnbooks without music. On their last wagon journey from Hebron, Martin and Neher each had obtained a calendar from the druggist. It was a treasured item, not only listing months and days, Sundays and holidays, but also giving facts of the almanac: dates of full and quarter moons, what to do if a child drank kerosene, and other hints, all written of course in English. Any child was punished who tore it, whether out of curiosity, or while looking for something to play with. The calendar was hung at the highest and safest place on the wall for protection. Ludwig thought it invaluable. From it he could study a few English words and then be able to converse better with his English speaking neighbors the Crowleys. Neher liked to study about America and compare the country to Russia. He took a keen interest in studying the language, even though sometimes he grew impatient. But when he was studying he often became a different person. It brought out his sense of humor. He was a smart man, no doubt with his mother's brains, able to figure things out more quickly than most people, even though he also was high strung, forceful, commanding, and impatient of those who could not learn as fast.

Nobody remembered much about Christmas of 1910, for St. Nicholas had nothing in his sack. Jaegers invited Martins and Nehers to their place a few days after Christmas so the children could see a Christmas tree with candles, tinsel, and animal cookies sprinkled with red sugar hung on the tree. The second winter was hard for the two families, but not as bad as the last when 12 people had been crowded into a single box car. Martins lived in two rooms, a wood shanty pushed against a larger sod room, but Nehers had less space, only one earthen room with hardly any lumber. It depressed Christina to think that her sister

Sophie was better off than she, and she wished she could read as Sophie did. At least Ludwig had brought a German Bible and a couple of evangelical song books, from which, when Ludwig read and sang, she gained spiritual strength during these times of want.

Martins and Nehers both realized during this winter that they had not regularly been keeping Sunday a holy day as their parents had taught them to do in Russia. They had grown up to believe that if they did not worship God and rest on Sunday, God would punish them somehow. And so Fred Martin, feeling that he had been back-sliding, and Ludwig Neher remembering his mother's advice, both families decided to have prayer meetings on Sundays. Gradually other Germans from Russia neighbors joined them in each others' homes for Sunday afternoon gatherings, some trudging over snow, others on horseback or by horse-drawn stone boat. Better-off settlers arrived with family nestled in a home-made sled. Often more time was spent getting there than being there, but they were together.

The group sang, to a rhythmic beat, evangelical songs they had memorized in the old country. A leader kept the singing going, for hymn books with music were not common in those days. They discussed scripture openly, and a convert was apt to admonish others of their sins. Women went to their knees and cried their woes out to God, but if a woman spoke of her man's abuse, she was scolded then and there. These people realized how much they needed help beyond themselves. Getting together was their one human contact to ease loneliness. They were soothed and gained strength to endure another week.

First-year immigrants were frightened by frantic yelps and howls of hungry animals, especially coyotes and wolves, who often came close to people's houses to wail cries of anguish and sometimes attacked a human being or a calf or cow. Unless a man stood upright with whip or sturdy stick, a wolf showed not much fear to leave the grounds. Coyotes practiced different strategy, sneaking around and suddenly pouncing on small animals like domesticated rabbits or chickens. Waist high snow was an advantage, for it discouraged animals from attacking, but they howled anyway, and made people very nervous.

The winter of 1910-1911 was one of the most lonely times, a true initiation into the rigors of Dakota winters. The winter before, having twelve in the boxcar at Ashley was crowded, but there was company along with the hardship. Now Christina complained of feeling ill from the smoke and foul air in the one room with dirt walls and a stove giving out puffs of smoke. Rubbing clothes on a washboard, rinsing in water from melted snow and then slowly drying them piece by piece, such labor got the best of her good nature. She was irritable and scolded a lot and had little patience with the little ones.

IV. 1911: Pauline's Birth

Gradually winter ended, and solid snow banks turned to water. Christina took two-year-old Dilda for a walk while baby Odeela slept, and she felt invigorated by being outdoors. Like other homesteaders, Neher tried to turn over last year's fields with a one-horse, one-share plow, but the Bay could not pull the plow, whose share sank into the heavy loam. Disgusted and despondent, Neher went once again to Matt Crowley, and for the first time Matt saw Ludwig cry. Matt told Ludwig to wait a few days and he would be there with his rigging. Crowley helped Neher till, seed, and break new patches for planting. Crowley seemed rather to enjoy Neher's interruptions, despite the fact that they made him miss a day's work at his own ranch. It was the two little girls who drew him, for he loved to play with them. They were pleased just to grasp his forefinger and hold on for dear life. The softness melted Matt's heart.

Martins and Nehers quickly completed their first harvest of 1910. "Ich kann net gla-ava was so a-a ma-sheen do-oa kann" (I cannot believe what such a machine can do). All were excited—men, children, animals. Gratitude interrupted their habits of worrying. **"Wa-itza hemmer un brot kemmer ba-cha"** (We have wheat and can bake bread). For once, America looked good. The first harvest supplied enough grain for bread and a little more for money. But it was not sufficient to clothe the many children the Martins had to provide for for the coming winter. Neither was it enough for tools and machines to enlarge their farming. Martin remembered how he looked at more settled homesteaders and saw the many newer devices that were needed for the American way of farming.

Ludwig and Christina managed to thresh ten gunny sacks of wind-blown wheat before Christina took sick. The rest of the piles of raked grain Ludwig carried home, one pitchfork at a time, to make a new stack. He had hoped to find an established homesteader to move a threshing rig into his yard to complete the threshing of wheat and even some of the oats. In a shrill voice he had asked Herr Jaeger, not expecting this good man to do it.

There were times when Ludwig did not understand Jaeger, a man of few words but strong temper who turned red when something went against his plans. Once, when Martin and Neher wanted to acquire some more level homestead land that Jaeger also had in mind to purchase, Jaeger's quick temper wished those Russians farther north ("Die Roosen solten weiter gehen hin in die gegend"). Knowing full well that that was wild and hilly country, he now felt indebted to these families and realized their plight. And that was why he made a special effort to thresh for them, to make up for taking the better land for himself.

Eventually their second summer arrived, very hot, but the crop was fair. Life was hard yet challenging. Settlers used what Nature provided to keep alive. They chopped fence posts from tree clusters, selecting trees that were straight and sturdy, and built fences to protect grain fields from roaming cattle and horses. But before that Nehers needed a fence to keep cows in the yard, and two posts for a wash line. Fence wire had to be purchased or charged, and there never was enough money for household needs.

Building a henhouse was another project, and for this women hauled gumbo clay to mix with small stones. Christine used a flat sharp-edged stone to loosen and scrape gumbo, cupped the silty soil into a pail, then lugged it over prairie hillocks, often spilling some on steep hills. She had reason to rest, lying down on prairie grass, and fancying the clouds were baby-carriages, for she knew she was pregnant again and worried that she would miscarry. Scripture was understood to mean that it was a woman's duty to bear children and to work hard. Because of the great demand placed on men just to survive, some became severe and took out their anxieties on wives and children by rough treatment, often beating them. This was a way of life that now cannot be described to fourth, fifth, and later generations. There was general abuse of minors in the family, children and wives, and it was considered discipline according to the Bible. (Of course such severe discipline did not prevail in every settler household.) Nevertheless the man in the family held all the rights, often making things hard on women folk.

Christina remembered the prosperity of Groszliebental, where her family not only had enough for food and clothing, but her father presented each of his daughters with a pair of gold earrings as part of her dowry. Today Christina wished for food and clothing for her little ones, but instead she had to face the fact that they were poor, and that she again was pregnant and not feeling well. Frau Boehler had visited Christina and found her in "andere umschtaenda" (in a family way): "Ach, mir sen doe for desz, mir weiver" (We are here for this, we wives).

Autumn was dry, and fire broke out in the Elm Creek neighborhood, one that took days to control. Men, women and children were summoned to help fight it. Neher hitched Bay to the stoneboat and upon it set a barrel of water along with a number of gunny sacks. Christina dipped a gunny sack into water, and struck at the advancing flames, doing as the neighbors did. But her back ached and she became aware that her unborn child had dropped considerably since the day before, a sign that she would deliver soon.

Ludwig fetched Frau Jaeger and the two arrived in time for the good midwife to deliver the premature baby on October 10, 1911. Frau Jaeger named the baby after her own daughter, Pauline, and because she was convinced it would die, she performed proxy baptism, then wrapped the three-pound child in swaddling cloths which she had brought along. She injected into her mouth droplets of sweetened camomile tea. Frau Jaeger's daughter Pauline came to help Christina, who was to remain in bed for nine days, according to the belief that nine days was the time it took for the body to recover from childbirth. Years later, Pauline Jaeger Birkmaier told of her experience, that because there was no privacy in the house, she was not able ever to take her clothes off. "There was such poverty, I cannot describe it. It was no wonder my mother gathered everything she could take to help. I shall never forget."

But the baby lived after all, so that Ludwig and Christina had three babies in a period of two years and seven months. Then Elsie was born May 20, 1913; Louise on October 19, 1914; and finally a boy Edwin on December 21, 1916. By this time a kitchen built of lumber had been added to the rectangular sod room. The Martins had two more children, Martha and Albert. Babies came often, for it was considered necessary to raise a large family in order to have help with the work, even though mothers craved more time between births.

The Martin family continued more prosperous than Nehers. With a good supply of teenage boys and girls, Fred and Sophie Martin had better workers and more land and stock. They enjoyed luxuries, like wax candles at Christmas which the children in my own family were denied. I can remember Martha unwrapping red tissue paper and finding a lace trimmed pettycoat. It wasn't so much the pettycoat I minded, but the rustle of the bright colored paper. Our clan of growing girls were brought up to strict hard work, especially the two eldest, Matilda and Ottilia, who became field workers and received harsh treatment from Pa. They were expected to do as much work as a man. I didn't grow as quickly, and so was chore girl to help mother with domestic work, which I did not like, and often was slapped by my mother. I much preferred being outdoors, and was very curious, traits that brought much trouble to my relationship with my mother. But Nehers were not alone in being too strict with children and women: that was common practice among most homesteaders of all nationalities. There was a story about a man throwing a plate at his wife because she had not cooked some food just right. Frau Boehler commented that "females were for that, young or old, they were slaves, of inferior rating, and were subject to any kind of treatment due to a man being insecure about what life held in store for him and his family. He struck out, either in words or blows."

I have heard both my father and Uncle Fred Martin say that they would rather forget those terrible first winters of homesteading. "Mir kennz gar net mit worta erklaera; desz waren verachten zeita" (We cannot explain in words; those were desperate times.) But not all times were bad. There were good ones too as the years went by: the wholeness and fruits of the great outdoors, the times when Pa bought each of us a pencil box with a few crayons out of the goodness of his heart; the times he told stories that made everybody laugh; the times Ma hovered over us as we lay in high fever, bending over and saying "Ach, du lieves kind, du bischt jo so krank" (You dear child, you are so sick). Once there was nothing to eat but corn meal mush swimming in fat and Pa said if he couldn't eat it, then the children couldn't either. It was one of his moments of fair treatment. As we grew older, there were times spent around the organ, and how Pa relished singing along with his children; the times Pa taught us German scripture and led morning devotions; the many good meals Ma prepared from scratch. She taught us to be neat and clean.

In the spring of 1916 the Ludwig Neher family moved to the Bitterman farm, which my father bought from Frau Bitterman and her sons on my father's word of honor. No note was made, only a small cash down payment, according to what I was told.

Peet Bitterman had died and was buried in the Homestead Cemetery, two miles south of the Bitterman place.

The years that followed were marked by hard work. We moved into a three-room wooden house, a luxury for our mother. How well we remember how we were all crowded into the northwest bedroom when Anne was born, and by the time the last child, Clara, came, we had obtained an upstairs of three bedrooms and a cellar where Pa managed to install a coal furnace. Milking as many as 18 to 20 cows by hand and raising poultry and hogs were the family's way of survival. Horses and humans did the work. The two older girls worked like men, hauling hay and pitching bundles for the threshing machine. All of us cleared stones from new broken fields, and manured barns, part of the hard manual labor that was every-day work for us. We were raised strictly, scraping and digging coal, digging fence post holes and throwing hay up the barn stairs, and we grew up as did many children on the prairie.

Learning German was important. People thought that if you read Scripture in English, the Spirit of God could not reach you. We organized as the Johannes Gemeinde and attended Sunday School and worship services in the Elm Creek school house, the same school house we learned subjects in English during the week. The struggle to retain German—a beautiful language and the only one proper for God's word, according to people of German-related nationalities—caused much dissension among new settlers.

My father acquired two sections of land in Mercer County, brought it into cultivated grain fields, and lost practically everything during the Depression. All that work, and for what? For children, life promised better. On the whole we had good country schooling and the advantages of an open and free life on the prairie where we learned to work, to pray and to forgive.

What a hilly and wild part of North Dakota are the Knife River prairies our parents settled on! I have no regrets, nor ill-will. More important that they chose America! A thousand thanks and tears of joy. I love every part of the Knife River prairies.

America is a great country! Yes indeed.

(Top) Pauline Neher Diede.
The Neher family. (Front) Edwin, Ludwig, Clara, Christina, Anna. (Back) Matilda (bo[rn] Russia) Ottilia, Pauline, Elsie, Louise.